# THRILL
## SPORTS

### IN THE
### GREAT LAKES REGION
### by
### BILL BAILEY

- **Ballooning**
- **Hang gliding**
- **Paragliding**
- **Soaring • Paintball**
- **Scuba diving • Flying**
- **Orienteering • Skydiving**
- **Ultralights • Climbing • Windsurfing**
- **Bungee jumping**

*Other Glovebox Guidebooks*

**Ohio State Parks Guidebook**

**Cycling Michigan: 25 Routes in West Michigan**

**What's Cheap & Free in Michigan**

**Porcupine Mountains Wilderness State Park Guide**

**Lower Michigan's 75 Best Campgrounds**

**Michigan Zoos & Animal Parks**

**Michigan's Only Antique & Flea Market Guidebook**

**Making Healthy Tomorrows**

**Thanks, Dad. You Really Where a Wise Guy**

To order any of the above books,
call or write:

**Glovebox Guidebooks Publishing Co.**
**1112 Washburn Place East**
**Saginaw, Michigan 48602**
**1-800-289-4843**

# THRILL
## SPORTS

### IN THE
### GREAT LAKES REGION
by
### BILL BAILEY

**The Warning**

Thrill sports can involve considerable risk, and can result in damage to property, personal injury or death. In participating in any of the activities described herein, readers assume all risk of injury or loss that may accompany such activities. The publisher and author have no financial interest in any of the businesses listed in this book, and accordingly disavows all responsibility for injury, death or loss which may arise from a reader participating in the activities written about in this book. The publisher and author make no warranties as to the safety, competence, reliability, or security of any operators, instructors, programs or businesses listed herein.

Library of Congress

Cover design and interior art by Dan Jacalone
Editing by Christine Uthoff

*Thrill Sports in the Great Lakes Region*
by Bill Bailey
ISNB 1-881139-10-7

Published by Glovebox Guidebooks Publishing Company
1112 Washburn Place East
Saginaw, Michigan 48602
1-800-289-4843

Printed in the United States of America
10 9 8 7 6 5 4 3 2

# *Contents*

# Introduction

Thrills and adventure, by definition, involve the unexpected, a little risk, a lot of rewards, a thumping heart and a dry mouth. Thrills of all kinds turn some of us on, really on. These highly personal encounters can alter your state of mind, scramble your daily routine and offer a buzz in your shorts that becomes powerfully addictive and pretty wonderful.

In fact, according to psychologist Marvin Zuckerman of the University of Delaware, people with a high need for sensation have lower levels of a brain chemical called momoamine oxidase (MAO) than people who aren't so inclined to live on the edge.

Zuckerman has been studying people he calls "sensation seekers" for 30 years, and has determined that even three-day-old babies with low MAO levels are more active and more "emotionally reactive," which means it takes longer to soothe them when they start crying. So, it seems some of us are born thrill seekers — and maybe crybabies; others have to learn it the hard way.

Exhilaration or terror? It's different for each individual says Michael Apter, author of *The Dangerous Edge: The Psychology of Excitement* (Free Press, $22.95). Apter says in order for many of us to feel exhilarated we need both the possibility of danger and a **"Adventure is a human need..."** belief there is protection from it. The protection can be our skills, training or the people around them. In short, say most researchers, if thrill sports weren't dangerous, they would not appeal to us. The challenge is using skill, training, quality equipment, and common sense to get your kicks and keep on ticking.

Great Lakes is a terrific region to explore the part of you that wants more: that part of you that wants to exchange dreams for real-life adventure; that part of you that is searching for ways to live each minute and each second as fully as possible. Whether you want to climb, fly, jump, travel, swim, use the winds, or soar the skies, this book can show you how to get started.

Adventure is a human need. Thrill sports — most of which are really quite safe and sane with proper training, exercise and good judgment — offers that great chance to ride exhilaration as the eagle flies the ridges, to feel almost too alive plunging into new skills, new adventures, and new ways to experience life.

The humble mission of this book is to introduce you to 13 or so thrill sports readily available in the Great Lakes, report the facts — not fiction — of the activities, and to give a general overview in easy to understand chapters. You'll quickly learn that each of the thrill sports, once broken into bite-size pieces, really are within the reaches, financially and physically, of just about anyone who wants some adventure in their lives. You can do it.

You'll learn about state of the art instruction and equipment, places to go, suppliers, outfitters, certification requirements, pitfalls and joys.

You'll also learn that you should always begin with a top professional; that thrill seeking takes commitment and skills; that there is a risk, you can die; and that you should let others, who are willing to pay the ultimate price, explore the outer limits of thrill sports.

Manage the risk, practice well-established safety techniques, use the best equipment and instruction and have a thrill.

*Battle Creek International Balloon & Air Show Championship*

CHAPTER 1

# Ballooning

You don't feel the wind when ballooning, because you are moving with it, at its will — sometimes skimming the tree tops at a fast walking pace, more often floating silently over rich farm fields and along the outskirts of heaven. Ballooning has been popular for centuries and is actually the first form of flight, but its magic has only recently been shared with the average person.

Today, recreational ballooning offers a colorful spectacle and serenity, punctuated only by the occasional roar of the gas burner heating the air that helps the huge envelope (which is the term used to describe the air-filled balloon) escape gravity and earthly concerns. From Africa to Egypt and over the Great Lakes, specialty operators offer tours and training; while many communities, such as Battle Creek, Michigan, host huge annual air shows and ballooning championships. There's much opportunity for novices to get hooked, join a club, or buy a balloon, and find with each landing a sip of champagne to celebrate the almost sensual experience.

The adventure comes with some unpredictability. Between 25 and 50 percent of flights are postponed or rescheduled because of winds exceeding 10 knots, fog, rain, rapidly changing weather systems or even snow. Don't give up, after a try or two most operators will launch you into one of aviation's most addictive sports. Set your alarm clock, the best ballooning is early, really early in the morning, before mid-day winds sweep the land and people become busy with their humdrum earthbound lives.

## Becoming a Balloonist
*From the basics to a balloon pilot's license*

### The Basics

Slung under the 50- to 80-foot-tall balloon, usually made of nylon or polyester fabric and coated with a mixture of polyurethane to seal and protect the air bag, is a wicker basket (called a gondola and sometimes constructed of aluminum or exotic plastics) and a giant propane burner that resembles a Bic lighter on steroids. The deafening sound of the burner, which heats the air that propels the balloon upward, is blasted with regularity to control altitude. To descend, the pilot may either let the envelope of air cool on its own or let the hot air spill out from a vent at the top of the balloon. As much as 20 gallons of propane can be burned during a two-hour cross-country flight.

The huge balloon lies flat on the ground, a wrinkled heap of nylon, until — with the help of as many as eight normal-sized ground crew members (or four jumbo-sized helpers) — a giant blower huffs and puffs air into the opening to make room for that first blast from the burner. The hot air quickly fills the envelope and the entire balloon soon stands upright. Helpers then hang on and steady the craft.

Straining at it's tethers, the balloon quickly fills with the light, hot air and is ready to be propelled by only the winds. Only gentle winds. About a 10-knot breeze is as much wind as allowed for the recreational ride. During the typical two-hour flight you may fly 10-12 miles and ascend to more than 2,000 feet above sea level. You can go higher, but why? The view and gentle passage of the craft over the earth allows a perspective unknown in other aviation endeavors. Some pilots glide at treetop levels, occasionally exchanging shouts from eager children who race to touch the shadow of the balloon. At other times, the crew floats up to 2,000 feet and looks down upon gliding birds, rooftops, and the checkerboard of farm fields and city lots.

Although there's no direct method of steering an enormous balloon — it will only drift along with the prevailing winds — skilled pilots can often take advantage of different winds at different altitudes and guide the floating giant along a particular path. That is, after they find a wind that blows the way they want to go.

## Training and Your License

Our friends at the Federal Aviation Administration (FAA), those zany guys whom many accuse of taking the fun out of sport aviation, regulate balloons, much like fixed-winged aircraft. No longer do fixed-wing pilots or balloonists fly or float around the patch, they must — and rightly so — adhere to a variety of rules and regulations designed to separate aircraft in the sky and protect the public.

Therefore, you, an excited future balloon pilot, must slow down a bit, find an instructor, and go through the certification process requiring a minimum of 10 hours of flight training with at least one hour of solo flight. Usually about 15 hours of actual air time are required by the average private student before he or she is ready for a check flight by an FAA examiner. Fledgling balloonists are also required to pass an FAA written exam that covers many federal aviation rules and requirements: rules of balloon operation, weather, and other laws and safety questions germane to safe flight over public lands. Every two years the pilot must renew his or her license by giving a check ride to an examiner and demonstrating proficiency and safe flying techniques and attitude.

> *Most students can complete training in a summer at a cost of $2000-$4000*

Most students can complete the training in a summer at a cost between $2,000 and $4,000 if the balloon school provides all equipment, including a chase team. If a serious student provides his own balloon, chase team and vehicle, the cost is merely the instructor's hourly rate and the training drops below $1,000. Shop around for a school, compare prices, and look for a full-time instructor.

## Balloon Buying Tips

Because the average balloon ride can cost $125 to $150 a person (or more) for a two-hour flight and often flights must be booked a week, if not a month, in advance, more and more enthusiasts are seriously considering buying their own equipment.

*A small gas powered fan helps inflate the envelop.*

True love ain't cheap — and it ain't simple. You need a balloon, burner and basket, and also propane fuel tanks, inflator fan, flight instruments, charts, trailer, champagne and at least $10,000 to $12,000 which buys a very basic used outfit. Brand new quality equipment packages start at $15,000 to $20,000, but you can easily spend $50,000 or more depending on specialized equipment, customized envelope design, and so on.

> "...the best balloons are made in the Great Lakes area."

Like any sport equipment, you pretty much get what you pay for, so when purchasing a balloon be sure to have some of these features: Kevlar cables, UV coating on fabric, polyurethane treatment, fireproof skirt, a quality basket, and necessary instruments that include an envelope temperature gauge, variometer (vertical speed indicator), fuel pressure and quantity gauge, and altimeter. AM radios are frowned upon.

The Great Lakes region is actually a very popular place for ballooning, instruction, and maybe most importantly construction of balloons. Two of the three largest balloon manufacturers are located in Michigan: Cameron Balloons, P.O. Box 3672, Ann Arbor, MI 48106, (313) 426-5525 and Thunder & Colt, 4017 East Baldwin Rd., Holly, MI 48442, (313) 695-5115. Both offer superior quality and terrific customer service and sales. West of the Great Lakes is Aerostar International Inc., 1813 E Avenue, Sioux Falls, SD 57117, (605) 331-3500.

The average sport balloon should have a capacity of at least 70,000 cubic feet with load-tapered seams for the gores (panels), quality fittings, and a record of safety that can be obtained from balloon insurance underwriters. Larger balloons with envelopes of 150,000 cubic feet will be more expensive but will allow you to carry more passengers. If you are considering buying a used balloon, learn all you can from salespeople, research reliability, and always review the balloon's annual inspections records and log books.

Okay, you bought a balloon, studied hard and passed your written exam. You still have not sustained all the costs of ownership and operation. While being a millionaire is helpful in most thrill sports, your main costs of operation such as fuel, insurance, depreciation of the envelope, inspections, simple maintenance, and occasional additional training can be shouldered by the average guy.

The average envelope — if given meticulous maintenance — can last for up to 400 flight hours. Normal annual use is about 50 flight hours. Including inspections and factoring in depreciation, your direct costs are nearly $4,000 annually. On top of those fixed cost, you have propane at about a buck a gallon (the burner will use about 10 gallons an hour depending on weather), insurance at $600 to $800 annually, chase vehicle and trailer, miscellaneous transportation costs, training, biennial flight checks, and other small expenses. It's all part of financing the airborne hobby.

## Balloon Services
Flights, Instruction, Tours

### *Michigan*                                        .

**Grand Traverse Balloons**
Traverse City, MI

(616) 947-7433

Owner Jeff Geiger operates three balloons that can take two to six passengers for rides over Grand Traverse Bay and Old Mission and Leelanau Peninsulas.

**Free Indeed Balloons**
Holland, MI
(616) 335-3363

Flights are planned for 60-90 minutes and lift off near Lake Michigan, between Grand Haven and South Haven. Great scenery!

**Michigan Balloon Corp. of America**
Burton, MI
(800) 969-8368

Departs from Seven Lakes State Park where you can camp, swim and fish. Five balloons hold two to eight passengers. Bed and breakfast packages available.

**Michigan Balloon Corp.**
Kalamazoo, MI
(616) 327-6446

Sunrise ascensions are a specialty, to view lakes and peaceful ponds, rolling lush farmlands, and experience quiet gliding over rural areas. Rides are 60-90 minutes long.

**Capt. Phogg Balloon Rides**
Fenton, MI
(313) 629-0040

*Ballooning is "Grrrrreat!"*

Eight balloons can handle two to eight passengers with flight patterns taking in 50 lakes in a 10-mile radius. Reservations are required two weeks in advance and bed and breakfast packages are available.

## HOTAIRBUS
Rockford, MI
(616) 874-7222

"Splash and dash" is Ron Korsky's specialty. "There are over 30 lakes in the area and I can skim the surface without getting my passengers damp." Three balloons, two to five people.

## A-1 Sky High Hot Air Balloons
Caledonia, MI
(616) 891-8520

Doug Mills has flown balloons for more than 20 years and flies in Africa during the winter. His fleet of eight balloons hold up to six people who often see dozens of deer in the rolling hills and streams in this part of the Great Lakes region.

## Up, Up & Away
Okemos, MI
(517) 347-1717

Each flight ends with the traditional champagne toast; Early morning flights end with a continental breakfast. Two balloons are dispatched to gently sail above mid-Michigan wildlife and countryside.

## Riverview Balloons
Hastings, MI

(616) 948-8847

Treetop flights are their specialty, offering excellent chances to see wildlife and the small lakes that are scattered along the rolling terrain.

## Wicker Basket Balloon Center
Walled Lake, MI
(313) 624-5137

Open Memorial Day through Halloween, veteran pilots depart from several locations depending on the winds of the southeastern Michigan location. Four balloons carry four to six passengers.

## Renaissance Balloons
Brighton, MI
(313) 229-7400

Specializes in carrying passengers over the "world's most wonderful, undeveloped countryside — Island Lake Recreation Area, Kensington Metropark, and surroundings." Group outings can be arranged.

## Upper Winds
Niles, MI
(616) 683-3036

Upper Winds operates three balloons over Michigan's wine country, along the Lake Michigan dunes, and over the St. Joseph River. On a clear day you can see Chicago!

## *Ohio*

**Clear Sky Balloon Port**
6929 Tylersville Rd.
W. Chester, OH 45069
(800) 733-2053

**Balloon Tours of America**
P.O. Box 723
Kent, OH 44240
(216) 673-6777

Ohio's biggest balloon operator with nearly 20 years of experience. Open seven days; champagne flights are available.

**Ad Venture Aloft, Inc.**
2695 Cypress Way
Cincinnati, OH 45212
(513) 351-5656

Sales, rides, training.

## *Pennsylvania*

**Dillion Hot-Air Balloon Service**
850 Meadow Lane
Camp Hill, PA 17001
(717) 761-6895

## Organizations and Clubs

**Balloon Federation of America (BFA)**

P.O. Box 400
Indianola, IA 50125
(515) 961-8809

## Books

The Art of Hot Air Ballooning, by Roger Bansemer, $35.95 from Gollum Press, 2351 Alligator Creek Rd., Clearwater, FL 34625

Ballooning, the Complete Guide to Riding the Wind, by Dick Wirth Random House, New York, NY

Taming the Gentle Giant, by Immogen Norwood $15.95 from Land O'Sky Aeronautics, P.O. Box 636, Skyland, NC 28776

## Magazines

Skylines
P.O. Box 1703
Portales, NM 88130
(515) 562-2412

Ballooning, the Journal of the Ballooning Federal of America
P.O. Box 51
Post Mills, VT 05058
(802) 333-4883

## Great Lakes area events

Battle Creek, (MI) International Balloon Championship &

Air Show — July 4th weekend, 150 balloons, events at the W.K. Kellogg Airport, 237 North Helmer Rd., Battle Creek, MI 49015-2019, (616) 962-0592.

Cincinnati (OH) Annual Balloonfest — Memorial Day, 60 plus balloons, (513) 752-6700

Glen Falls Balloonfest (NY) late September, (518) 761-6366

Jackson, (MI) Hot Air Jubilee — Third week in July, 50 balloons, (517) 782-8221.

# CHAPTER 2

# Bungee jumping

**It** was great while the fad lasted. Too bad bungee jumping is fading from the thrill seekers list of pursuits. Fewer and fewer bungee operators or event sponsors are offering bungee jumping due to accidents, saturation of the market — after all, how many times in one lifetime do you want to pee your pants while falling to the earth — and the high cost of insurance and overall lack of profitability.

"Bungee puts blood into your head," says Neil Nitschka, a veteran thrill seeker. "If your heart doesn't skip a beat and you don't scream on the way down...and thank God on the way up...you ain't alive."

Bungee jumping is a no-brainer thrill sport. Just show up with a fist full of money, strap on the elastic cords, and Geronimo! There are no lessons or certificates — other than a few witty remarks from the operator, no expensive equipment, no written tests and no surly instructors. "In that brief moment of weightlessness, just before the recoil, you'll be glad you came," says Nitschka. It's simple, safe if you carefully choose an operator, and maybe the wildest minute in your life.

## Reverse Bungee — The Slingshot

After careful calculation of the "death vs. bungee cord recoil distance," some Great Lakes bungee operators are offering the "slingshot," or reverse bungee, where friendly employees, usually five large guys in black T-shirts, attach the stretchy cord to your back then hold you as the jump cage is raised and the bungee cords stretch and stretch until they can't hold you any more.

Snap! They let go, and if all the calculations are correct, you won't splat against the bottom of the jump cage. "Zoom," says Nitschka, "is the best way to explain it, seeing the sky come at you is refreshing, but the bottom of the jump cage looks awfully big on your way up, too."

> *"The wildest minute in your life..."*

"What's great about the rebound or slingshot bungee experience is that you don't have to decide to jump," says Nitschka a veteran of many jumps and slingshots.

Currently few insurance companies and even fewer operators are endorsing reverse bungee jumping. Shop carefully for this thrill.

## Getting Hooked

Although not found in the Midwest, bridge or BASE jumping, even leaps from balloons, are offered in other parts of the country and all require very safe equipment. The connections to you and the launch platform must be secure, and the cords must be in good condition and correctly calculated for your weight. All connections — harness and fasteners to cords and platform should be doubled. Redundant safety features are critical.

> **"Check the 'death vs bungee' recoil distance"**

The most common type of harness and method of attaching the bungee cord is a chest/waist harness that allows the cord to be connected to your front. This harness is considered to be the best for beginners and safely allows the transfer of "G-force" to your hips.

Less common, the mid-body harness allows the cord to be securely connected to your back, and you can then make a face first dive. More exciting, but there is the rare chance that jumpers who faint could block their airway when their head slumps forward.

"Ankle jumps are increasing in popularity," according to Nitschka. "Diving off the platform in a perfect swan dive is a terrific rush... It's actually better than drinking several beers and peeing off the porch." Remember a couple of common sense safety rules will help make your "swan dive" safer, preventing your body from elongating too much, too fast.

First, keep your knees bent slightly, letting the large muscles in your legs take some of the shock; second, practice front-connected jumps until you get the feel of the shock point; and third, seek tall jumps so you can enjoy a longer flight and longer deceleration.

## Walk the talk

In many states bungee operators are regulated under various amusement ride regulations and are inspected by the state. However, you should ask about and visually inspect equipment, ask to see operators permit, call the state office that regulates amusement rides, and so on, before taking the big step off the platform.

Ask what type of bungee cords are used. There should be several cords, usually 5/8-inch or 3/4-inch in diameter with a strong rubber core, cotton interbraid, and dense nylon sheath that protects against UV rays and abrasion. A 5/8-inch cord has a 1,000-pound load capacity, while the 3/4-inch cord can hold about 1,400 pounds.

Always expect the operator to use five times the load placed on the cord by your weight. In other words, if you weigh 150 pounds, the operator should use three 5/8-inch cords. The three cords should be sheathed together to prevent tangles during rebound.

## More Questions for Operators

Do you have insurance? How long have you been in business? Have you had any accidents? Injuries? How old are the bungee cords? Do you have many bungee cords and harnesses that can be used for many different sizes of jumpers? How many staff members, and what are their duties and experience levels? Are the cords carefully handled and protected from sun and abrasion? What is their load limit rule (strength and stretch — it should be 5 to 1 loading or more)? Are all attachments redundant?

## Where to go

"If you find a qualified bungee operator in the Great Lakes, take the plunge but be ready for a gape-mouthed experience. A stomach twisting dive, then a moment of weightlessness at the top of the rebound, and a exhilaration like none other as you yo-yo at the end of the cord, at the end of the jump," says Nitschka.

> *"...a moment of weighlessness at the top of the recoil..."*

Some fairs, festivals, and summer recreation areas have bungee operators, but as mentioned they are getting harder to find. Even state travel bureaus don't keep track of operators, but many local convention and visitor bureaus or regional travel associations may be able to direct you to lodging and jumping opportunities.

*Indoor climbing walls are popular teaching and practicing locations in the Great Lakes area.*

CHAPTER 3

# Climbing

Climbing is the world's original thrill sport. Centuries before parachutes, planes, paragliders, or other motorized thrills, man climbed bare-faced cliffs for kicks. Scaling higher and higher over faces of ice and rock, early climbers used "free" climbing, a type of technical climbing that exposes you to a fatal fall. Today's "free" climbers use only natural "holds," but more and more usually use protection (some ropes and mechanical mounts) only enough to save their lives.

"Aid" climbers always use protection, such as mounted anchors, carabiners and ropes, to prevent falls, not to propel them up the rock or ice face.

As a beginner, free climbing is divided into two types: top-roping and lead climbing.

Top-roping is the style of climbing beginners are taught under the supervision of a skilled teacher. The beginners are always attached to a rope, which is safely connected to the top of the climb. If you make a mistake, which I did every two-and-one-half minutes, you don't fall very far, you merely "come off the wall." The belay rope, which is solidly anchored, prevents you from falling more than a couple of feet. Your pride is the only thing that drops.

Lead climbers are talented and experienced climbers capable of selecting and placing rope-anchor points as they move upward. Beginners and all other climbers below the lead climber have their safety in his or her hands.

Although there are some excellent climbing opportunities in the Great Lakes region, sport climbing, which can take place indoors or out, is typically a shorter climb, often using pre-set protections that allow for a more aggressive and mentally exhilarating climb. Sport climbing is truly a dance with the mountain or cliff, where safety and fun is the goal for all ages and skill levels.

## Kindergarten for climbers

Virtually all of the indoor climbing facilities listed later offer introductory rock climbing lessons, which often last from one to three hours and can cost $30 to $75 depending on the length of wall time. Many gyms also offer weekend courses focusing on movement skills, supervised practice times, and the use of harnesses, ropes, and so on. Beginning indoor climbers often master basic skills faster than outdoor climbers simply because they get more practice.

Typically, lessons begin with a talk detailing climbing terminology, equipment, how to communicate between climbers, logistics of climbing, environmental issues, and safety, safety, and more safety.

Outdoor lessons will include placing and setting and installing top-ropes. The instructor will show you and allow you to place anchors above the climbing route, explaining how to choose set points and the use of mechanical anchors.

After some discussion about the value and need for strength-building exercises and stretching, you'll learn about harnesses and knots. Soon you'll know how to buckle on a harness, double back on a buckled harness and how to safely tie into the top rope.

From ground level you'll learn basic belay methods, including anchoring techniques, rope handling, rope braking and the use of braking for belay devices, communication, and general rope use and safety.

To build confidence and your technique, your instructor will start you on easy outdoor routes on non-vertical rocks, and on low-level indoor walls. And, of course, once you and your partner become skilled, balanced, and strengthened, you'll graduate to more difficult routes.

## The language of climbers

**Belay.** The belayer usually stands at the bottom holding onto the rope that is looped through a friction device and through the belayer's harness. Belayers carefully take up slack as you climb. If the climber falls, the belayer can quickly put the brakes on by using the friction device, causing the rope and the climber to stop.

**Screamer.** A long fall whereby small patches of your flesh may be left on the wall.

**Pumped or blown.** When the climbers muscles are heavily exerted and filled with extra blood. Fatigue.

**Top Rope.** The rope is carefully laced or looped through nylon webbing and carabiners, which are anchored at the top of the wall or cliff. Climbers attach this rope to their harness and as a climber ascends the belayer takes up slack in the rope. The farthest the climber could fall is the total length of the slack plus slight rope stretch.

**Solo Climbing.** No protection (rope) is used, this is the most dangerous form of climbing.

> *A screamer:*
> *a long fall*
> *whereby small*
> *pieces of*
> *flesh are left*
> *on the climbing*
> *wall*

**Lead Climbing.** For the experienced, strong climber. The skilled climber wears a harness attached to the rope and puts "protection" equipment into the cracks and crags of the cliff face every five to 10 feet as he or she ascends. The rope is then attached to the protection as the climber goes up. As the climber ascends, the belayer plays out slack, but if the lead climber falls while five feet above his or her last protection, they fall 10 feet plus rope stretch.

**Bouldering.** Primarily a practicing exercise whereby climbers use no ropes or harnesses while hanging onto the rock face and moving laterally.

**Harness.** Constructed of durable and strong nylon webbing, it's worn like a diaper around the legs, butt, back, and waist.

The climbing rope is attached to the harness.

**Climbing Shoes.** The soles, which wrap around the feet, are very tight and made from a soft black rubber that grips and flexes.

**Carabiners.** Usually referred to as "beaners," the O-shaped, pear-shaped and D-shaped metal rings have a locking mechanism that is used on harnesses and in anchoring ropes to the cliff top.

**Flashing.** A fast climber.

**.Elvis or Sewing Machine legs.** This happens when your legs are overexerted and begin to shake and twitch, and "dance" as Elvis Presley once did.

## Equipment

Both indoor and outdoor schools typically provide equipment for introductory free-climbing lessons. All you will need is a pair of climbing shoes, often called "sticky" shoes. Carabiners, harness, and rope will be provided. Many climbing schools will also require a helmet for outdoor work.

**...you'll need a pair of "sticky" shoes and "beaners"**

As with most thrill sports, quality equipment is essential. The best equipment will be tested to UIAA (Union International des Associations d'Alpinisme) standards, which is your guarantee the equipment is safe. Make sure the equipment you use at school is well maintained. Always inspect any

equipment before you attach it to yourself. Visually inspect ropes for fraying, harness web and buckles, helmets, and make certain your climbing shoes fit.

## About schools/instructors

As a beginning rock climber your best investment is in a quality instructor, someone you trust and a person dedicated to your safety and needs. Because your instructor (and other climbers) literally have your life in their hands, try to find experienced teachers and climbing partners that share your interest in safety and serious fun.

Because there is no instructor or climbing school certification body that is widely accepted, you may search for a member of the AMGA (American Mountain Guides Association), a fairly new group that is trying to implement a certification process and program for climbing teachers and schools.

In short, AMGA wants to standardize instruction and requires that AMGA members have proper insurance, operate using correct permits, and are experienced and active.

## Places to Climb Indoors

### *Illinois*

**The Sporting Club**
211 N Stetson
Chicago, IL
(312) 616-9000

**Gravity**

1935 S. Halstead
Chicago, IL 60608
(312) 733-5006

**Hidden Peak**
1780 N. Marcey Place
Chicago, IL 60614
(312) 335-1200

**Midwest Rocksport**
108 First St.
Batavia, IL 60510
(708) 879-8889

**Upper Limits**
1220 37th St.
Peru, IL 61345
(815) 224-3686

## *Michigan*

**Benchmark**
32715 Grand River
Farmington, MI
(313) 477-8116

18-foot-high wall is open and free to the public. Beginners must request instruction. Open 10 a.m. to 9 p.m. weekdays, 10 a.m. to 5 p.m. Saturday, and noon to 5 p.m. Sunday.

**Inside Moves**
6391/2 76th St. SW
Grand Rapids, MI 49509

(616) 281-7088
Open weekday evenings and Saturdays from 10 a.m. to 4 p.m.
Fees are $7 during the week, $8 on Saturdays. Lessons, $30.

**The Ultimate Sports Bar**
40 W. Pike St.
Pontiac, MI
(313) 253-1300

**Starr Commonwealth Schools**
Albion, MI
(517) 629-5591

Open to the public 5 to 9 p.m. Tuesday-Thursday, 4 to 8 p.m.
Saturday, and 3 to 8 p.m. Sunday. It costs $7. Located in the
Outdoor Adventure facility.

## Minnesota

**Peak Adventure**
9208 James Ave. S
Bloomington, MN 55431
(612) 884-7996

**Vertical Endeavors**
844 Arcade St.
St. Paul, MN 55106
(612) 776-1430

## New York

**City Climbing Club**
533 W. 59th St.

New York, NY 10025
(212) 408-0277

**ACC Gymnasium**
P.O. Box 850
Susquehanna Ave.
Cooperstown, NY 13326
(607) 547-2800

**Hard As A Rock Training Center**
630 Glen St.
Queensbury, NY 12804
(518) 793-4626

**Lindseth Climbing Wall**
Cornell University
P.O. Box 729
Ithaca, NY 14851
(607) 255-1807

**Climb Manhattan Plaza Health Club**
482 West 43rd St.
New York, NY 10036
(212) 563-7001

**Rockworks**
1385 Vischer Ferry Rd.
Clifton Park, NY
(518) 373-1215

*Ohio*

**Benchmark**

Columbus, OH

**Miami University Climbing Wall**
Withrow Ct. Gym
Oxford, OH 45056
(513) 529-2360

## Pennsylvania

**Basecamp**
723 Chestnut St.
Philadelphia, PA 19106
(215) 592-7956

**The Climbing Wall Inc.**
7501 Penn Ave.
Pittsburgh, PA 15208
(412) 247-7334

**Climbnasium, Inc.**
339 Locust Point
Mechanicsburg, PA 17055
(717) 795-9580

**Climb On**
1206 N. Sherman St.
Allentown, PA 18103
(215) 435-4334

**Exkursion**
4123 William Penn Hwy.
Monroeville/Pittsburgh, PA 15146
(412) 372-7030

### Mountain Creams International
1121 Bower Hill Rd.
Pittsburgh, PA 15243
(412) 276-8660

## Places to Climb Outdoors

### Grand Ledge-"The Ledges"
City of Grand Ledge, Michigan
Near M-43 and M-100
(517) 627-2383

40-foot sandstone ledges located off of Front Street on the
north side of the city in Oak Park.

### Halton Region Conservation Area
Milton, Ontario
Southwest of Toronto
(416) 336-1158

There are 60- to 80-foot cliffs at Rattlesnake Point and Kelso
Crags, a four-hour drive from Detroit, Michigan.

### Bruce Peninsula National Park
Tobermory, Ontario, in Georgian Bay
(519) 596-2233

50- to 90-foot cliffs in a 36,000-acre park with 240 campsites.
Call ahead for information about camping and special activities in the park.

### The Shawangunks (The Gunks)
New York

(914) 658-9811

**Devil's Lake State Park**
Baraboo, WI
(608) 356-8301

**Big Bay — Bud's Wall Climbing Area**
30 miles northwest of Marquette, Michigan.

Take County Road 550 toward Big Bay, turn left onto County Road 510, turn right onto triple A Road and go about one mile, then turn right onto a two-track dirt road.

**Keweenaw Peninsula**
Houghton, Michigan

# Instruction

**University of Michigan Outdoor Recreation Program**
(313) 764-3967

Classes held at Grand Ledge, Michigan.

**Vertical Ventures**
922 W. Willow St.
Lansing, MI
(517) 485-7681

Beginner and intermediate courses provide instruction on top roping at Grand Ledge, Michigan. Trips around the Great Lakes are also offered.

**Side Treks**

P.O. Box 7131
Marquette, MI
(906) 228-8735

**Adirondack Alpine Adventure**
P.O. Box 179
Keene, NY 12942
(518) 576-9881

Broad range of ice and rock climbing instruction.

**High Angle Adventures**
5 River Rd.
New Paltz, NY 12561
(800) 777-2456

20 years of experience, superb rock wall instruction, plenty of hands-on supervised practice.

**High Impact Adventures, Inc.**
Madison, WI
(608) 222-7343

Courses offered at Devils Lake State Park for $60 to $100.

# Climbing Outfitters

### *Illinois*

**Active Endeavors**
522 Dempster
Evanston, IL 60202
(708) 869-7073

**Mountain Tops**
228 West Main St.
St. Charles, IL 60174
(708) 513-7603

**Shawnee Trails**
222 W. Freeman
Carbondale, IL 62901
(618) 529-2313

**Upper Limits**
1220 37th St.
Peru, IL 61354
(815) 224-3686

## Michigan

**Inside Moves**
4384 Air West
Grand Rapids, MI 49512
(616) 698-7449

**Benchmark**
32715 Grand River
Farmington, MI
(313) 477-8116

## Minnesota

**Midwest Mountaineering**
309 Cedar Ave. So.
Minneapolis, MN 55454
(612) 339-3433

**Sportsman's Headquarters**
17 W. Superior St.
Duluth, MN 55802
(218) 722-6858

## New York

**Outdoor Traders**
Westchester Ave.
Pound Ridge, NY 10576
(914) 764-0100

**Tents & Trails**
21 Park Place
New York, NY 10007
(800) 237-1760

## Ohio

**Action Haus**
4166 S. Cleveland-Massillion Rd.
Norton, OH 44203
(800) 231-HAUS

**Aquanetics Outdoor Pursuits**
144 E. Olentangy
Powell, OH 43065
(614) 848-6663

**Great White North**

1309 Ridge Road
Hinkley, OH 44233
(216) 278-2449

## Pennsylvania

**Climb On**
1206 N. Sherman St.
Allentown, PA 18103
(215) 435-4334

**Exkursion**
2123 William Penn Hwy.
Monroeville/Pittsburgh, PA 15146
(412) 373-7030

**Mountain Dreams International**
1121 Bower Hill Rd.
Pittsburgh, PA 15243
(412) 276-8660

**Top of the Slope**
100 S. Main St.
Wilkes-Barre, PA 18701
(717) 822-6627

**American Sport Climbers Federation**
(212) 865-4373

**The American Mountain Guides Association (AMGA)**
P.O. Box 2128
Estes Park, CO 80517
(303) 586-0571

# Books and Magazines

Hard Rock: Masters of Stone II, by Eric Perlman Productions, 1993, ($29.95).

Knots for Climbers by Chris Luebben, 1993, $3.95. Chockstone Press, P.O. Box 3505, Evergreen CO 80439.

Mountaineering — the Freedom of the Hills ($19.95), from the Mountaineers (800) 533-HIKE.

Rock & Ice Magazine (monthly, $12.50) P.O. Box 3595, Boulder, CO 80307, (303) 499-8410.

Face Climbing, by John Long, Chockstone Press.

Snow and Ice Climbing, by John Barry ($16.95) from Alpenbooks, Box 761, Snohomish, WA 98260. 160 pages.

Basic Rockcraft, Royal Robbins, from LaSieta Press (1989).

Mountain Magazine (England) P.O. Box 184, Sheffield, S119D1, England. Published six times a year.

Climbing Magazine (monthly) P.O. Box 339, Carbondale, CO 81623, (303) 963-0372. Since 1970.

Learning to Rock Climb, Michael Laughman 1981 ($12.95) Sierra Club Books. Great book for beginners, offers introduction to terminology and techniques.

Sport Climbing Connection Magazine, P.O. Box 3203, Boulder, CO, (303) 442-5242.

How to Rock Climb, by John Long, 1989 ($9.95) For beginners by Chockstone Press.

Michael Chessler Books, P.O. Box 4267, Evergreen, CO 80439. Largest collection of climbing books in the country. Free catalog.

## Videos

Moving Over Stone, Light Productions, P.O. Box 2906, Mammoth Lakes, CA 93546.

Basic Rock Climbing, Vertical Adventures Productions, P.O. Box 8188, Calabasas, CA 91372, (818) 883-4921.

Climb International ($19.95) Video Action Sports, Inc. (800) 727-6689.

Other videos available from Video Action Sports, Inc. include: Moving Over Stone II; Climb; Masters of Stone; Basic Rock Climbing; Art of Leading; KNOW Limits and others.

On the Rocks and Over the Edge, OTR, Box 93974, Los Angles, CA 90093, (213) 466-4921.

Training to Rock Climb, The Vertical Club, (206) 283-8056. Workouts, strength training.

Sierra Club Books. Great book for beginners, offers introduction to terminology and techniques.

Sport Climbing Connection Magazine, P.O. Box 3203, Boulder, CO, (303)442-5242.

How to Rock Climb, by John Long, 1989 ($9.95) For beginners by Chockstone Press.

Michael Chessler Books, P.O. Box 4267, Evergreen, CO 80439. Largest collection of climbing books.

*From a flight around the patch to heart-pumping aerobatics, flying is an increasingly popular thrill sport.*

# CHAPTER 4 Flying

Once a person has skillfully ventured into the sky alone and returned gently, that person is forever changed. Fulfilled in only a way other pilots can appreciate. Private pilot flying is on the increase. From the shade tree mechanic building high-tech experimental aircraft to the thousands each year that go it alone, flying can be affordable and as thrilling as you want to make it.

## Around the world in 38 days

The big adventure, which I call *'Mark & Dave's Excellent Adventure,'* was actually the result of a smaller adventure in 1987 they flew the nasty north Atlantic in a single engine aircraft. Michigan professional pilot, Mark van Benschoten and college professor Dave Bledsoe flew 2,500 miles following a route over Canada, Hudson Bay, Greenland, Scotland to Ireland, armed with hand-held radios and cold water survival suits, and no global positioning navigational aids, and no fancy equipment like they took on their next trip.

"That trip went so smooth," van Benschoten said with a wink, "that we immediately shocked our wives with the planning details and news of our global circumnavigation." The intrepid duo convinced their nervous spouses that a small loan of several thousand dollars, clean underwear, new navigational radios, and a 120-gallon gas tank installed where the back seat used to be, was all that was needed for a safe trip.

Dave Bledsoe, who reminds you of David Letterman and Michael Palin, was the official handyman on the trip. He rigged an old fishing reel that would spool a flexible antenna out a hole in the bottom of the airplane, to more exactly tune in the short wave radio when they were hundreds of miles from a transmitting station. Van Benschoten says Dave will do anything to tune in a clear "oldies" AM radio station.

"We flew over jungles, desserts, ice caps, the Alps, dusty towns that looked like a fly speck, big sprawling congested cities that got uglier the closer you got, and back to Bay City, Michigan, our home base, that, by the way, never looked so good after 38 days wedged into a single engine Mooney M-20F," says van Benschoten. "Unlike flying in the US, where there are about 12,000 small airports scattered everywhere, navigation for a around the world flight was our biggest concern, our greatest achievement, and a testament to the new satellite navigation system that can pinpoint your location anywhere in the world."

"Some of our best memories included our futile effort to win vast sums of money in Reno, a camel ride...the camel survived our threats, the beauty of Greenland, scuba diving in the clear warm waters of the south Pacific, a crocodile dinner with an

*Dave Bledsoe and Mark van Benschoten flew around the world in 38 days in a single engine Mooney.*

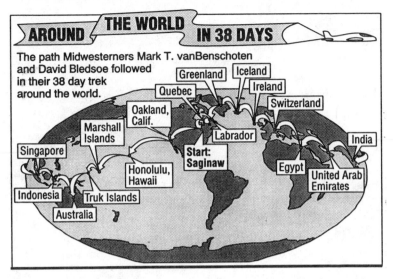

**AROUND THE WORLD IN 38 DAYS**

The path Midwesterners Mark T. vanBenschoten and David Bledsoe followed in their 38 day trek around the world.

- Greenland
- Iceland
- Ireland
- Quebec
- Oakland, Calif.
- Marshall Islands
- Switzerland
- Labrador
- India
- Singapore
- Start: Saginaw
- Egypt
- Honolulu, Hawaii
- United Arab Emirates
- Indonesia
- Truk Islands
- Australia

Aussie that caused surprisingly little retching, smaller Hawaiian islands and the friendliest airport on our journey located in Ireland," says van Benschoten.

The trip also included stops in Singapore, United Arab Emirates, Egypt — with a hilarious tour of the pyramids, Labrador, India, Switzerland, the Marshall Island, and all points between.

"After four years of talking, and one year of planning, the trip completely filled our expectations, even on the down side. The worst part of the global tour was dealing with certain custom officials in developing counties," says Bledsoe. "They were slow, expensive and painful...sometimes you felt like getting out of the plane and simply bending over the wing, if you get my meaning."

"Bribery," says van Benschoten, "is the only thing to call it. Officials would sometimes call it landing fees, or processing fees, but in short it was bribery. Almost like a food chain, each airport official seemed to get a piece of you. In some cases we spent more than $200 to clear the way for our departure."

Both pilots are regular guys — with a big loan to pay off — that insist what they did is no superhuman feat, but an adventure requiring good basic training, common sense, planning, and attention to detail. All of which just about anybody could duplicate. In short, private piloting can be a Sunday afternoon spin around the patch, or as for Dave and Mark, a trip of a lifetime covering 20,000 miles of ocean flying, landings in foreign countries, urinating in a bottle during 16-hour legs of the flight, and eating dozens of cans of tuna fish. It's your choice, thrill seekers.

> **What's next for the intrepid boys?**
> **A polar circumnavigtion (maybe)**

What's next for the fly boys? "Dave and I have been eating many breakfasts together lately," says van Benschoten who is the best of friends with Bledsoe, "planning, yes...we are in the planning stages for a polar circumnavigation. Dave is already thinking up new stupid plane tricks we can amuse ourselves with."

## Primer

Aside from the thrills — especially if you advance to aerobatics or long mountainous cross-country flights in a small plane — there are actually many sane and logical reasons to learn to fly. Flying can free you from highway hassles, let you set your own itinerary, and open more than 12,000 airports not served by commercial carriers; but most importantly, it puts lift under your wings and clouds at your side, freeing you in almost spiritual ways that few ground dwellers can understand or bother to attempt.

## How much does this fun cost?

Not as much as you might think. In fact, a private pilot's license, which includes plane rental, ground school, and dual instruction time, costs about $3,000 to $3,500 and could take a couple of months to a year to complete, depending on your schedule and the weather. Prices are usually higher near big cities.

## Getting your license

If you can read, speak and understand English, and if you are 16 years old and in reasonably good physical shape you can hold a student pilot certificate, which allows you to fly solo as part of the private pilot training course. (Glider and balloon pilots can begin at age 14.)

Your first step toward the cockpit is to pass a simple physical exam given by an FAA approved physician. Your local flight schools have a list of approved doctors in your area. The physical is pretty routine and most people pass, unless you suffer from diabetes, epilepsy or some other incapacitating ailment. As long as your vision can be corrected to 20/30 or better, wearing glasses is fine. You must also be able to distinguish the colors red, green, and white.

Once you pass the physical, which, by the way there is no age limit to take, you'll be given a Class III medical certificate. It is wise to take the physical before lessons, just in case you have a hidden or restricting malady.

## How long does it take?

The average student pilot living in the Midwest and battling ever-changing weather systems, should expect taking about six months to complete the private pilot's license requirements.

Depending on the type of flight school you attend you'll need to complete a minimum flight time of either 35 or 40 hours before you'll be able to take the private pilot's check ride. The average of student hours logged before the FAA check ride is about 70, according to statistics.

Our friends at the FAA, the gods of flight, require 40 hours of flight for certification and stipulate how that time should be spent. Half, 20 hours, must be in flight instruction, with at least three hours completed in cross-country flights and a least three hours at night. The remaining 20 hours (or more) must be composed of at least ten solo cross-county flight hours.

Most local airports, and the closer the better, have flight schools. Ask all of the obvious questions. Ask for references, meet the instructor, check with former students, and look for an overall sense of quality and professionalism. There are also flight schools, usually located in southern states, that offer concentrated courses so you can virtually complete training in a long, but busy vacation.

The more planes a school operates, the better your chance of

scheduling a plane when you want it. Make sure the school provides ground training; although many community education departments also offer evening ground schools. Weekend ground school and home study courses and videos are excellent ways to reinforce your skills and learn the technical material in your own home, at your own pace.

## There is a lot to learn

But you can do it! In fact, if you can drive a stick shift car, you probably have the motor skills to fly a small airplane.

You learn the theory of flight on the ground, then practice it in the air with a certified flight instructor. Typically, ground school classes begin with a general explanation of the components of an airplane and how they make it fly.

*Pretty soon the mystique of flying will be replaced with factual knowedge...*

Ground school is packed with information about FAA rules and regulations, as well as a good fundamental background in the physics of flight. You'll understand lift and weight, thrust and drag and heading, power setting, fuel burns, chart reading, communications, and virtually a new language of aviation terms. Pretty soon the mystique of flying will be replaced with factual knowledge — and that's good.

## Flying the plane

After your physical and early in your ground school training, your instructor will start teaching the basics of maneuvering

— taxiing, takeoffs and landings (which aren't as difficult as you might expect).

Navigation skills, using the onboard radios, weather, and flight planning, will be integrated into your early flight hours; and as you gain experience, the actual handling of the aircraft becomes increasingly easy and natural.

Much of the dual instruction time will be devoted to precision flight — learning to maneuver the aircraft through turns, controlled climbs and descents.

## The Solo

As soon as you've completed 12 hours of dual flight instruction (often a little longer), your instructor will approve your first solo.

*After the solo, students begin a rapid increase in their skills...* This is a major step toward your private pilot certificate, confidence building, and a turning point in your aviation career. Often after the solo, students begin a rapid increase in their skills and begin practicing diligently as they begin closing in on the hours needed to complete the private pilot course.

This is also the time when many students choose to take the FAA 60 question written examination. The multiple-choice test covers FAA regulations, weather, navigation, various aviation-related calculations, and general aviation knowledge relating to the operation of a small private plane.

# You are a pilot

You've passed the written test, completed flight instruction, and passed a check ride with an FAA certified examiner. You can now carry passengers and share expenses with them, but you can't fly for hire or reward. You'll also still be limited to flying in good weather. Many private pilots immediately launch into training for their instrument rating, which when completed allows them to fly in various weather conditions and generally makes them a safer, better pilot.

The instrument rating allows pilots to fly when weather provides less than the optimal visual conditions to which students have so far been limited.

You have to log 40 hours of instrument training, and you can't take the instrument flight test until you have a total of 125 hours. As with the private pilot license, you'll be required to pass a written and flight test.

Aerobatics training, which can lead to some big-time thrills complete with snap rolls, spins, high angle turns, and much more, can begin after a couple hundred hours of flying. Aside from the thrill of the maneuver, many experienced pilots believe that some aerobatics training — especially spin training — is the best insurance policy available.

Aerobatics training requires specially certified instructions and aircraft. Novice competitions, thrills, and a strong social life are the hallmark of aerobatics enthusiasts.

CHAPTER 5

# Hang gliding

Although most instructors usually start fledgling hang glider pilots on flat ground, teaching handling techniques for the overhead wing, the first flight off the "bunny hill" is a memorable introduction to the purest form of flight. You're in the air (maybe only inches into the air), usually on the second day of training, and you're suddenly becoming tuned in, to the breezes and weather patterns, to the wonderful skill and to the joy of soaring birds barely noticed just a day or two ago. Depending on your skill, you'll be flying on longer, higher, and more exciting flights each day out.

The first successful attempts at flight were made by hang glider pilots Otto Lilienthal, Octave Chanute, and, our pals, the fearless Wright brothers. In fact, the Wright brothers were successful powered-flight inventors because of their hang gliding mastery. Unlike the utilitarian-powered flight that has been perfected through the century and transports us anyplace in the world if you have the money, the thrill of "free flight" or gliding isn't the destination — it's the trip.

Sport hang gliding has been boosted by new technology during the past twenty years. Today's extra light and durable craft fly better, faster and farther than anything the Wright brothers ever dreamed of. Pilots must be well trained and skillful to meet the demands of today's equipment, and elements. Surrounded by those elements, hang glider pilots easily cruise to 10,000 feet, soaring for hours and equipping their high performance gliders with ballistically-launched parachutes for added safety.

## Becoming a hang glider pilot

"Your first flight can be off the bunny slope, where in a few hours of supervised practice you'll begin to trust the winged device and your skills," says Bill Fifer, certified instructor and owner of Traverse City Hang Gliding/Paragliding in Traverse City, Michigan. "The short, hop-like flights are only a few feet off the ground and you learn to do basic techniques and land safely on your own two feet."

A tandem flight is maybe the quickest and best way to experience hang gliding. Tethered to a specially certified instructor and slung under a two-person craft, the teacher can launch the glider and take you on a 20 minute flight, perform some basic maneuvers, and turn over the controls to you as your heart pounds and interest soars.

Flights vary in height and distance depending on the condition and site, and can cost less than $100 for the initial tandem ride. You will soon determine if that first effort stirs your sense of adventure enough to take up the challenge of formal lessons. As with all forms of aviation, hang gliding requires a serious commitment. For additional information on training and certified instructors, contact the United States Hang Glider Association, P.O. Box 8300, Colorado Springs, CO 80933, (719) 632-8300 or fax (719) 632-6417.

## Schools and instructors

More than nine out of 10 student hang glider pilots abandon the sport long before they are certified, according to Fifer. "Many students stay long enough for a few flights, seemingly getting their kicks and a lasting memory, never to return to the sport...and that's fine, a thrill that will last more than a lifetime. Others, I'm convinced, have a poor experience at a poor quality school or with a bad instructor." Fifer has been training hang glider pilots for 15 years and urges novice hang gliders to find: high quality, experienced USHGA certified instructors; quality facili-

> *"A tandem flight is maybe the quickest and best way to experience hang gliding."*

ties with gentle bunny slopes that are flyable in a variety of wind conditions; video training tapes; small class sizes; and compatibility with your instructor.

The price of training is also an important consideration. Most top schools offer some type of fee structure that includes a total or maximum price for the type of rating you seek. In short, they will guarantee all the lessons and access to equipment it may take to obtain a certain rating or level of skill.

"Quality equipment of recent vintage and HGMA (Hang

Glider Manufacture's Association) certified gliders complete with wheels that ease landings for beginners are a must," says Fifer. All hang gliders are subjected to extensive structural and aerodynamic testing, assuring strength under load and during maneuvers. "Some schools do modify their beginner (bunny hill) hang gliders to make them a little smaller and lighter for students."

The lighter and slightly smaller gliders are fine for student use, making them easier to lug around, as long as they are used under supervision on the beginner slopes. These smaller hang gliders can also be used for general flying.

Finally, quality schools will offer extensive ground schools that provide a thorough curriculum covering flight theory, weather, equipment care and use, flight manuals, emergency procedures, site discipline (tips on when and where to fly safely), and loads of safety instruction.

In short, look for schools that use up-to-date equipment and treat you in a professional, valued-customer manner. "Professionalism is probably the element that separates the quality, safety-driven flight schools from the fly-by-night operators," says Fifer who's been in business since 1970 and also operates a small shop.

Traverse City HG/Paragliding is the only full-time provider of instruction in Michigan. "Look for strong manufacture support, too," Fifer says. "Talk with as many active pilots as possible and remember that most good schools turn out a respectable number of active pilots who have good safety records."

# USHGA Organizational Directory

## *Illinois*

**Raven Sky Sports**
Brad Kushner
Chicago, IL
(312) 360-0700

**High Expectations HG**
Dan Hartowicz
15 Westfield
DesPlaines, IL 60018
(708) 699-8545

**Air Wear Sports**
Larry Capps
P.O. Box 1094
Herrin, IL 62948
(618) 942-5317

**Spectrum Hang Gliding**
Angelo Mantas
5116 Pratt
Skokie, IL 60077
(708) 679-5338

## *Indiana*

**Kentuckiana Soaring**
Mike Kelley
425 Taggart Avenue
Clarksville, IN 47129
(812) 288-7111

**JJ Mitchell Hang Gliding**
John Mitchell
6741 Columbia
Hammond, IN 46324
(219) 845-2856

**Airborne Sails of Indiana**
Richard Sacher
6 Sylvan Lane
Jeffersonville, IN 47130
(812) 288-6597

## *Michigan*

**Great Lakes Hang Gliding**
Jay Darling
9746 Karen Court
Bridgman, MI 49106
(616) 465-5859

**Pro Hang Gliders**
Norm Lesnow
569 W. Annabelle
Hazel Park, MI 48030
(313) 399-9433

**Michigan Soaring Supplies**

Doug Coster
6531 Platte Road
Honor, MI 49640
(616) 882-4744

**Traverse City**
HG/Paragliding
Bill Fifer
1509 E. 8th Street
Traverse City, MI 49684
(616) 922-2844

## New York

**Schutte Sails/Swing USA**
Bob & Gayle Schutte
170 E. Main Street
Arcade, NY 14009
(716) 492-4576

**Wings and Wheels**
Paul Yarnall
2440 Brickyard Road
Canadaigua, NY 14425
(716) 394-8651

**Center of Gravity Harness**
Jay Gianforte
R.R. 173
Chittenango, NY 13037
(315) 687-3724

**Ultra Flight Systems**

Bob Murphy
15 Dean Street
Deposit, NY 13754
(607) 467-3110

**Mountain Wings, Inc.**
Greg Black
150 Canal Street
Ellenville, NY 12428
(914) 647-3377

**GMI Paragliding**
Philippe Renuadin
P.O. Box 451
Glen Cove, NY 11542
(516) 676-7599

**Land, Sea & Air
Hang Gliding**
Eric McNett
5957 E. Seneca Turnpike
Jamesville, NY 13078
(315) 492-1020

**Wing Sails by
Gunnar Graubaum**
Finkle Road
Millerton, NY 12546
(518) 789-6550

**Susquehanna Flight Park**
Dan Guido
7 Catherine

Mohawk, NY 13407
(315) 866-6153

**Aerial Adventures**
Peter Fournia
28 Woodlyn Way
Penfield, NY 14526
(716) 377-0535

**Fly High Hang Gliding, Inc.**
Paul Voight
R.R. 2 Box 561
Pine Bush, NY 12566
(914) 744-3317

## Ohio

**North Coast Hang Gliding**
Mike Del Signore
1916 W. 75th Street
Cleveland, OH 44102
(216) 631-1144

**Skyward Enterprises**
Mario Manzo
2259 S. Smithville Road
Dayton, OH 45420
(513) 256-3888

## Minnesota

**Skyline Skydogs**
Dan O'Hara

2719 Lindahl Road
Duluth, MN 55810
(218) 624-4500

**Sport Soaring Center**
Pat Caulfield
2074 Vienna Lane
Eagan, MN 55122
(612) 688-8218

**Ballistic Recovery
Systems, Inc.**
Dan Johnson
1845-HG Henry Avenue
South St. Paul, MN 55075
(612) 457-7491

## Pennsylvania

**Valley Forge
Hang Gliding**
Jeff Frelin
150 N. Bethlehem Pke
#A302
Ambler, PA 19002
(215) 643-4782

**Mountain Top Recreation**
Jeff Hostler
224 Rodlin
Pittsburgh, PA 15235
(412) 697-4477

**Windwalker Hang Gliding**
Darl Gearhart
R.R. 2 Box 2223
Schickshinny, PA 18655
(717) 864-3448

**Wind Spirit Hang Gliders**
Joe Miller
845 Central Avenue
Southampton,PA 18966
(215) 357-6026

**Wind Drifter**
Richard Cobb
623 W. Foster Avenue
State College, PA 16801
(814) 867-8529

**Sky High School of
Hang Gliding**
Bill Umstattd
733 Stoke Road
Villanova, PA 19085
(215) 527-1687

## *Wisconsin*

**Glide Path**
Martin Bunner
1107 88th Avenue
Kenosha, WI 53144
(414) 859-2777

**Air Magic**
Neil Roland
1915 Wood
LaCrosse, WI 54603
(608) 781-6113

**Water Specialties**
Wayne Colden
N3945 Nichols Creek Road
Waupaca, WI 54981
(715) 258-3951

**Raven Sky Sports**
Brad Kushner
P.O. Box 101
Whitewater, WI 53190
(414) 473-2003

# Training & your license

The average USHGA pilot, if there is such a thing, is 38 years old, has an average income of $44,000 annually, is married and went to college. Nearly 92 percent are male. How are we doing? Whether you fit this typical pilot description or not, everybody must obtain certain skill levels and basic knowledge before you are certified as a beginner pilot (Hang 1 level).

The USHGA has five pilot ratings, called the "Hang" system: Hang 1 (Beginner); Hang 2 (Novice); Hang 3 (Intermediate); Hang 4 (Advanced); Hang 5 (Master). Flying sites are also classified according to this system.

"Quality hang gliding schools will be aimed at getting students to the Hang 1 level, which allows student pilots to fly over gentle slopes using low altitudes," says Fifer. "Typically a Hang 1 program will cost about $400, but we always encourage pilots to obtain a Hang 2 rating...which makes a safer pilot and qualifies you to take higher altitude solo flights." Each rating level is a safety measure. Obtaining the Hang 2 rating can take 10 to 20 lessons and cost up to $800. "Pilots should progress to the Hang 2 rating as soon as possible," insists Fifer. Most students can progress from Hang 1 to Hang 2 in about 15 hours.

To achieve Hang 2, you must be able to make a smooth 90-degree S-turn over preselected points, land within 40 feet of a designated target, demonstrate controlled flight and pass a written examination. The Hang 2 rating allows you to fly 300 feet above ground and in winds up to 18 mph. You may now leave the bunny hill.

"Learning to fly a hang glider is really a fairly simple set of motor skills and anyone with reasonable strength and fitness can be a pilot in a few weekends," says Fifer. After a few hours of comprehensive ground school you'll make many runs on level ground, then on the first day at the bunny hill you'll likely make 15 or so trial takeoffs, each lasting about 15 seconds.

> **"Learning to fly a hang glider is really a fairly simple set of motor skills..."**

"Most beginners will find the first couple days pretty humbling," according to Fifer. "Managing a 30-foot wing isn't easy, it feels awkward, heavy and the harness is restrictive. Even with the best instruction you won't feel smooth and you might be discouraged in the very beginning. The good news is that the learning curve is rapid and each flight gets easier, more controlled and longer."

Soon you'll earn your Hang 1 rating, which allows for a maximum 150 feet altitude over gentle open slopes.

Experienced instructors agree that rating progression from Hang 2 to Hang 3 is the most difficult because much of the skills must be self-taught while in flight. For years this frustrating trial and error method without instructor guidance meant a long learning curve and often discouraged pilots from increasing their rating and skills level. Now, tandem training has changed the way pilots achieve skills and ratings. An instructor is harnessed with you under an oversized wing where student and teacher can learn and practice advanced methods.

*Launching in Traverse City, Michigan.*

Training time is reduced dramatically with tandem flying; in fact, most Hang 2 pilots need only five dual lessons to master Hang 3 skills, but another 20 hours of practice are needed to attain certification.

## Buying your hang glider

Congratulations, you are a Hang 2 pilot, you had 20 or more lessons and maybe 50 hours of flying and you're addicted to the sport. It time to buy your own wings. A basic single-surface design hang glider can cost about $1,500 new, but as a Hang 2 pilot who promises to take more lessons and study hard, you might be ready to move up to a double-surface glider that could cost as much as $2,500 new, or can sometimes be found used for less.

Always flight test prospective gliders, talk with dealers and other owners and look for the HGMA Certification of Compliance placard.

## Manufacturers

**Moyes California**
752 B Casiano Drive
Santa Barbara, CA 93105
(818) 887-3361

**Pacific Airwave**
P.O. Box 4384
Salines, CA 93912
(408) 422-2299

**Seedwings**

41 Aero Camino
Goleta, CA 93117
(805) 968-7070

**Torrey Pines Gliders**
10343 Rosselle Ste. 9
San Diego, CA 92121
(619) 457-4454

**UP Int'l**
4054 W. 2825 North
Mountain Green, UT 84050
(801) 876-2211

**Wills Wing**
1208 E. Walnut
Santa Ana, CA  92701
(714) 547-1344

# Organizations

**United States Hang Gliding Association (USHGA)**
P.O. Box 8300
Colorado Springs, CO 80933
(719) 632-8300 Fax: (719) 632-6417

# Books and Magazines

Hang Gliding Flying Skills, by Dennis Pagen, ($9.95), is a 12-chapter, USHGA approved training manual, used in most flight schools and as the training text of thousands. From Sport Aviation Publication, P.O. Box 101, Mingoville, PA 16856.  Also from this publisher is Understanding the Sky,

($19.95); Hang Gliding Flying Techniques, ($6.95); Paragliding Flight, ($19.95); and books on ultralight training.

Right Stuff for New Hang Glider Pilots, Erik Fair, ($8.95). Available from USHGA.

Hang Gliding Magazine, the official publication of the USGHA, P.O. Box 8300, Colorado Springs, CO 80933. Published since 1971 and the 1985 Maggie Award winner, Hang Gliding Magazine features up-to-date articles, advertisements, and skills improvement information.

Hang Gliding for Beginning Pilots, by Pete Cheney, ($29.95). More than 260 pages and 160 easy-to-understand illustrations and photos. USHGA books, call (719) 632-6417.

Downwind, by Larry Fleming, ($10.95), from Gregor Publishing, Dept. G, P.O. Box 26595, Fresno, CA 93729-6595.

Higher Than Eagles, by Chris Wills, ($19.95), is the life and times of hang gliding legend Bobby Wills. USHGA books.

## Videos

New York Finger Lakes Region Video, ($29), a 54-minute guide to sites, towing, and this entire New York area. East Coast Video, 80 E. Lincoln, Muskegon, MI 49444.

Hang Gliding Extreme, ($34.95), is 50 minutes of cross country flying, balloon drops, tow trucks, and interviews with world record setters. Informational and entertaining. From Adventure Video, 4750 Townsize Road, Reno, NV 89511, (702) 849-9672.

Sierra Cloudbase II, ($29.95), is 90 minutes of race and site guidance. Includes a visit to an aerobatics festival and lots of action. Also from Adventure Video.

Thermion — The Art of Flying, ($49.95), is 40 minutes of step-by-step instruction explaining all aspects of hang gliding from safety to meteorological conditions. Also from Adventure Video.

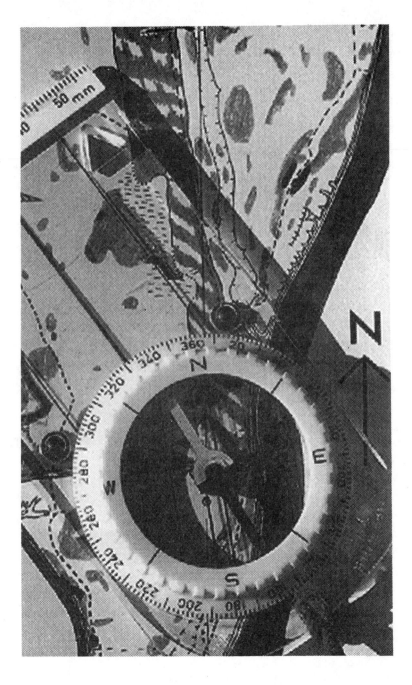

# CHAPTER 6 Orienteering

Orienteering is a foot race, a puzzle-solving thought race, a cross-country running sport and a potentially rugged event that takes participants — depending on their skill level — to remote and isolated areas where thinkers and outdoorsman are challenged by nature, navigation, and the elements.

Orienteering is a treasure hunt and a track meet combined, only there is no track — just rocks and hills and trees and streams, and a course so tricky you'll need a map to follow it. To win you'll need a compass, map skills, fitness, sharp thinking, outdoor skills, and foot speed.

You are the sport. It's elegant and simple, and can be a real thrill to successfully navigate difficult courses or place in the top ten.

Orienteering is a series of checkpoints that racers (or joggers or walkers) must reach before crossing the finish line. With no exact course set, participants must figure out the fastest route around boulders, bogs, brush and other natural obstacles using only their wits, maps, and compass.

## Which way do I go

"The sport's objective is to locate markers in the woods using a very detailed topographic map and compass," says Jon Nash, Director of Marketing and Public Relations for the U.S. Orienteering Federation. "Competitors navigate through the woodlands or over fields and park lands to reach a series of sequentially numbered checkpoints which are often orange-flag-marked sites called controls. Attached to the marker, which is usually attached to a large tree or rock, is a card which runners must punch to prove they were there."

> *Orienteering is a treasure hunt and a track meet combined...but there is no track...just rock, hills, and trees...*

"Competitors race against the clock, starting one at a time at intervals of about three minutes," says Nash, a veteran competitor. "Everybody has the same map, and events often have many different course layouts for different skill levels."

"There are always at least three different good routes between you and where you need to get to on a course. Choosing the right course is where the map reading and strategy skills come into play.

Take a wrong turn and finding the next checkpoint can be disorienting and very difficult," says Nash.

# The course

Courses are laid out by experienced orienteers and regional club members. The courses vary from location to location, but you can always count on some rugged terrain. First, according to the USOF, maps of the areas are drawn based on aerial photographs, a process called photogrammetry. The base map shows elevations, contours, density of plant undergrowth, and other features such as roads, trails and even large buildings.

"Then a field inspector walks the course, checking for accuracy, dangers, and adding detail that can only be gained by hiking the route," says Nash. Special features are noted, the map is drafted, and a legend is added that helps competitors interpret the area.

# The history

Over 800,000 people annually participate in organized orienteering events worldwide. In 1988, orienteering was accepted by the U.S. Olympic Committee as a Group C sport. From corporate executive training at local events — and one day the Olympics — orienteering's roots are in Scandinavia and the military.

"There's about 35,000 people in the U.S. who orienteer," says Nash, "and it's growing, with the USOF membership surpassing 7,000."

"As the sport grows, it is changing. In fact, courses are becoming more challenging, some offering increased problem solving issues and natural obstacles. Plunging through swamps and across creeks, and up and down rugged hills, is rapidly making orienteering a thrill seekers sport, if they can take it."

# Organizations

## *Illinois*

### Chicago Area Orienteering Club
George Bryson
111 E. Elm St.
Wheaton, IL 60187

### Southern Illinois Orienteering Club
Ken Ackerman
RR #10 Box 25
Carbondale, IL 62901

## *Indiana*

### Wandering Hoosiers Orienteering
c/o David Boes
Box 1622
Indianapolis, IN 46206
(317) 386-2502

## *Michigan*

### Southern Michigan Orienteering Club
Paul Shank
2307 E. Jolly #15
Lansing, MI 48910
(517) 887-8506

## *New York*

**Hudson Valley Orienteering**
Jon Nash
P.O. Box 61
Pleasantville, NY 10570
(914) 941-0896

**Buffalo Orienteering Club**
Dave Cady
148 Humboldt Parkway
Buffalo, NY 14214
(716) 837-3737

**Long Island Orienteering Club**
John Pekarik
238 Loop Dr.
Sayville, NY 11782

**Orienteering Unlimited Orienteering Club**
Ed Hicks
Jan Ridge Road
Somers, NY 10589
(914) 248-5957

**Rochester Orienteering Club**
Linda Kihn
874 Edgemere Dr.
Rochester, NY 14612
(716) 865-2161

**Central New York Orienteering Club**
Laurie Collinsworth

321 Ringwood Rd.
Freeville, NY 13068

**US Military Academy Orienteering Club**
Dept. of Geography
West Point, NY 10996

**Wilderness Orienteering Camps**
P.O. Box 202
Mahopac, NY 10541
(914) 628-7106

**Kodak Orienteering Club**
Kodak Recreation Bldg. 28
Kodak Park
Rochester, NY 14650
(716) 724-1837

**Empire Orienteering Club**
P.O. Box 51
Clifton Park, NY 12065
(518) 452-1346

## *Ohio*

**Northeastern Ohio Orienteering Club**
P.O. Box 37060
Cleveland, OH 44137
(216) 729-3255

**Orienteering Club of Cincinnati, Ohio**
Paul Crek
435 Probasco #4

Cincinnati, OH 45220
(513) 221-6213

**Miami Valley Orienteering Club**
Frederick Dudding
2533 Far Hills Ave.
Dayton, OH 45419-1547
(513) 294-2228

## *Pennsylvania*

**Indiana University of Pennsylvania**
IUP ROTC
Pierce Hall
Indiana, PA 15705
(412) 357-2700

**Susquehanna Valley Orienteering**
Michael Ball
5587 Mercury Rd.
Harrisburg, PA 17109
(717) 657-1833

**Land of Vikings**
270 Ehrhardt Rd.
Pearl River, NY 10965

**Warrior Ridge**
P.O. Box 191
Rice's Landing, PA 15357
(412) 883-2238

## *Wisconsin*

**Badger Orienteering Club**
748 W. Wisconsin Ave. #4
Peewaukee, WI 53072
(414) 691-9405

To start an orienteering club in the Midwest contact Pat Meehan, 1306 Southern Hills Blvd., Hamilton, OH 45013 or Al Smith, 74 Decorah Dr., St. Louis, MO 63146.

# Map Sources

**USGS Map Sales**
Box 25286, Federal Center
Denver, CO 80225

**USOF**
Teena Orling
911 Barnard College Lane
University City, MO 63130

# Books and Magazines

From United States Orienteering Federation
P.O. Box 1444
Forest Park, GA 30051

(Books and other orienteering supplies available from *A and E Orienteering,* 74 Decorah Dr., St. Louis, MO 63146 or *J. Berman Orienteering Supply Co.,* 248 Amherst Road #309, Sunderland, MA 01375)

Orienteering — The Adventure Game, ($5.50), by Lowry.
Be Expert with Map and Compass, by Bjorn Kjellstrom.
Coaching Orienteering, by Mary Jo Childs.

Orienteering Skills and Strategies, ($19.50), by Lowry and
Sidney.

Orienteering Training and Performance, ($19.50), by Lowry
and Sidney.

Armchair Orienteering, ($12.00), by Winifred Stott.

Teaching Orienteering, ($38.95), by McNeil, Ramsden and
Redfrew.

Orienteering Technique From Start to Finish, ($14.25),
Norman and Yngstrom.

Learn Orienteering, (70-cents), Silva Compass.

Cross Country Navigation, ($16.95).

Orienteering North America Magazine, ($20 annually).
23 Fayette St. Cambridge, MO 02139

U.S. Orienteering Team Newsletter, Fred Zendt, 355 Balboa
Ct., Atlanta, GA 30342. Step by step instruction explaining
orienteering.

CHAPTER 7

**P**aintball — with $CO_2$ powered guns sometimes called the "Brute-O-Matic," "The Stingray," or "Eliminator," camouflage, full-face goggles, knee pads, and the occasional welts — is one of the fastest growing participation sports. Unlike many other thrill sports, paintball games are team events, relying on strategies. Players work together to capture a flag or hill, or attack or defend a particular position.

High on natural adrenaline, players often call the sport, "safe danger," a challenging game played with a gun where you can shoot other people — and be shot by other people — and live to tell the tale over and over again. Like the animated characters in your favorite arcade game, you have many lives. With each game you live again, shoot again, and work together toward a goal using interdependence, skill, stealth, planning, and individual initiative in balance.

Aside from the skills needed for proficient paintball, players will also find themselves outdoor, often visiting new natural areas weekly to play the game, which will soon replace those vicarious thrills once brought to you by droning television shows and slick celluloid heroes of the big screen. You'll escape the weekday humdrum and replace it with vigorous sport: running, dodging, crawling, and tuning each of your senses to their highest levels. You'll squint to see your "enemy" while learning that no plan always works and that the script of the game changes with each heartbeat.

## Becoming a player

Although there are countless variations of the sport, the concept is basically this: a group of people head out into the woods, split up into teams and try to kill each other! Well, just about. Fortunately, unlike real guns, paintball guns shoot only a small, non-toxic, biodegradable paint pellet. Once hit, you're dead only until the next game, and the fun is endless as you stalk and get stalked by other armed players.

"Paintball is a very safe sport, gaining credibility and visibility as more and more players from every walk of life discover the challenges and thrills," says Rick Bolger, owner of Silver Lakes Action Sport Games in Brighton, Michigan. "Novice players, or anyone interested, are always welcome at game fields around the Midwest. The industry is working very hard at forming leagues for all ages and levels, and promoting the sport as a challenging game that can be played at any level of effort or seriousness." Bolger operates one of the oldest facilities in the region, featuring 300 acres with five playing zones.

> *"...players from every walk of life discover the challenges and thrills."*

Virtually all facilities offer daily rental of guns and supplies, but many fields require that you provide your own protective safety shield headgear. The headgear is often tested by the operators or referees to assure adequate protection. According to Bolger, you can visit and participate most weekends on your own, or better yet get a group of friends together and have a game. Owners, including Bolger, welcome new groups and will help with brief training and organization of the outing. Reservations are almost always a good idea.

## Training

Safety is the first and foremost concern of paintball game areas. Quality facilities require proper safety equipment and expect players to be in adequate physical fitness to endure the level of playing they are seeking.

Many clubs and facilities feature brief training on gun use, orientations to the competition site, and advise you on types of protective clothing that include knee and elbow pads, footwear, goggles, field hazards and so on. No license is required to buy paintball guns, however, age requirements vary by state. Paintball supply stores often offer gun safety and operation training, and as you will see later there are many books detailing all aspects of the sport.

> *Paintball supply stores often offer gun safety and operation training.*

"One of the most important things beginning players should learn is that protecting people is everybody's business, and that well structured and monitored games with strict rules make the sport safe and satisfying for the most competitive athletes," says Bolger. "Playing only on regulation fields, where there is trained staff, referees, and speed controlled guns is the best idea for all players."

Most facilities control the power or speed of the paint pellet to reduce the chance of injury beyond a mild sting. Bolger's game area tests often and requires that all guns shoot under 300 feet per second.

Daily equipment rental (gun, goggles, limited supply of paintballs included, etc.) can be under $20. Field rental is extra and based upon the number of players and the time rented.

## Equipment costs

"Most players can expect to spend $400 to $500 for a decent gun, goggles, and outer wear," says Bolger, who also operates a paintball warehouse club. "But as players become more involved and proficient, you can move up to more expensive or even custom-made $CO_2$ powered paintball guns, scopes, bulk loaders, travel, rip-stop clothing, and many smaller accessories that round-out the sport."

Paintball ammo costs about $6 to $8 per hundred and can also be purchased in bulk, where 2,500 pellets might cost as little as $125.

Four-hour playing field rentals vary but during tournaments and special events weekends many facilities offer a full day of play for under $20. Many facilities also have food concessions and player supplies on the grounds.

# Paintball fields, services

## *Illinois*

**The Adventure Game**
23 West North Ave.
Northlake, IL 60164
(708) 531-1413

**The Adventure Game**
3S 571 Winfield Road
Warrenville, IL 60555
(708) 393-3637

**Air America**
914 Greenwood Ave.
Glenview, IL 60025
(708) 998-8311

**Challenge Park**
Wilmington, IL
(708) 531-1413

**Bad Boyz Toyz**
15160/15164 LaGrange Rd.
Orland Park, IL 60438
(708) 301-1161

**Ballmeisters**
201 N. State Street
Chicago, IL 60411
(708) 757-3333

**Emperior's HQ**
5744 W. Irving Park, IL
Chicago, IL 60634
(312) 777-8668

**Fox River Games**
Naperville, IL
(708) 369-3225

**Bad Boyz Toyz**
17913 Torrence Ave.
Lansing, IL
(708) 418-8888

**JAS Military Supply**
1420 West Jefferson St.
Joliet, IL 60435
(815) 741-1622

**Master of the Game**
914 Greenwood
Glennview, IL 60025
(708) 998-8277

**MidwestAdventureGames**
1605 W. 1st Ave. Rte. 6
Coal Valley, IL 61240
(309) 799-5200

**Challenge Games**
Joliet, IL
(815) 729-1332

**Eagle Ridge Paintball**
Clinton, IL
(217) 935-5572

**Paintball Blitz**
Routes 41 & 21
Gurnee, IL 60031
(708) 998-8287

**Pneumatic Ordnance**
4118 Douglas Dr.
Zion, IL 60099-1330
(708) 746-4707

**Splat-Um Field, Inc.**
Greenville, IL
(618) 664-3230

**The Stealth Games**
Box 13
Cordova, IL 61242
(309) 523-3898

**Strange Ordnance**
914 Greenwood Ave.
Glenview, IL 60025
(708) 998-8312

**Paint Blast**
Decatur, IL
(217) 429-6677

**Wargames West**

Saint Anne, IL
(815) 932-1968

**Walter's Paintball Field**
Carrier Mills, IL
(618) 994-2200

**Action Games, Inc.**
Naperville, IL
(708) 554-2555

## Indiana

**Adventure Zone**
8641 East 116th St.
Fishers, IN 46038

**Dark Armies**
2525 N. Shadelands Ave.
Indianapolis, IN 46219
(317) 353-1987

**Indianapolis Army & Navy**
6032 East 21st
Indianapolis, IN 46219
(317) 356-0858

**KEA Combat Games**
RR 26, Box 353
Terre Haute, IN 47802
(812) 898-2766

**The Mill Paintball Game**

8990 Gore Road.
Bloomington, IN 47403
(812) 824-8125

**Blast Camp**
Waukesha, IN
(312) 486-1661

**Paintball Park**
1400 Estrelloa
Fort Wayne, IN 46803
(219) 749-1022

**Rat-A-Tat**
608 East Troy Ave.
Indianapolis, IN 46203
(317) 783-5562

**TnT Sporting Goods**
12822 Darlene Ct.
Granger, IN 46530
(219) 271-9345

## Michigan

**Action Outdoors**
1622 East Michigan
Jackson, MI
(517) 783-4434

**Adventure Connection**
Mason, MI
(517) 694-7555

**Allen Park
Paintball Supply**

6601 Park Avenue
Allen Park, MI 48101
(313) 388-5111

**Battlefield
Plaintball Game**
Jonesville, MI
(517) 694-4169

**The Battlegrounds**
Westland, MI
(313) 326-6096

**Bulleye Army Surplus**
4907 S. Division
Grand Rapids, MI 49548
(616) 530-2080

**DJ Paintball Paradise**
36335 E. Groesbeck Hwy.
Clinton Twp., MI 48035
(313) 790-1130

**Exotic Sportz**
Box 619, 123 Pearl St.
Pickney, MI 48169
(313) 878-2002

**Futureball Indoor/Out-
door Games**
Whitmore Lake, MI
(313) 231-0045

**Harry's Army Surplus**
201 East Washington
Ann Arbor, MI 48104
(313) 994-3572

**Hell Survivor, Inc.**
Box 619, D-19
Pickney, MI 48169
(313) 878-5656

**K & R Paintball**
Warehouse Club
28533 Greenfield
Southfield, MI 48076
(800) 597-0016 or
(313) 557-8256

**Lone Wolf Creek Paintball**
44750 Van Dyke
Utica, MI 48317
(313) 286-0562

**Lone Wolf Paintball**
Almont, MI
(313) 733-8844

**Midland Area Paintball**
Midland, MI
(517) 631-9503

**The Outpost**
23944 Eureka Road
Taylor, MI 48180

(313) 287-6460

**Paintballs and More**
21838 Vanborn Rd.
Dearborn Heights, MI 48125
(313) 563-6549

**Silver Lake Action**
Sport Games
Rick Bolger
9185 Silverside Dr.
Brighton, MI
(313) 469-9111

**Splatball**
Port Huron, MI
(313) 987-7528

**Splatball City**
8301 Epworth
Detroit, MI 48202
(313) 875-7549

**Splatball Survival**
Box 5385
Saginaw, MI 48603
(517) 799-7633

**Splatz Ltd.**
5578 Cooley Lake Rd.
Waterford, MI 48327
(313) 681-4411

**Supply Sargeant Inc.**
4907 South Division
Grand Rapids, MI 49548
(616) 530-2080

**Supply Sargeant Inc.**
8847 Portage Rd.
Portage, MI 49002
(616) 323-2266

**Surplus City**
1900 N. Wayne Rd.
Westland, MI 48185
(313) 721-2262

**Victory Paintball, Inc.**
Saline, MI
(313) 429-3147

**Wacky Warriors**
Imperial, MI
(313) 296-0964

**Wolverine Sports Field**
Escanaba, MI
(906) 786-7682

## Minnesota

**Action**
**Tag Paintball**
Rochester, MN
(507) 281-1804

**The Adventure Zone**
St. Paul, MN
(612) 571-8935

**Paintball Tag**
Zimmerman, MN
(612) 441-6862

**Splatball, Inc.**
Minneapolis, MN
(612) 788-6392

**Splat Zone Survival**
RR 1 Box 270
Mankota, MN 65001
(507) 278-4120

## New York

**Action Sports Outfitters**
23 North Main St.
Pearl River, NY 10695
(914) 624-2762

**Action Sports Outfitters**
Sunset Camp Rd.
Plattekill, NY
(914) 624-2762

**Aerostar East**
259 Hamlin Center Rd.
Hilton, NY 14468
(716) 964-7992

**American Air Gun Games**
Corman, NY
(516) 698-6230

**Army Navy Surplus**
1158 George Urban Blvd.
Cheektowaga, NY 14225
(716) 684-8728

**Assault Hill 1700**
Newark, NY
(315) 331-4980

**Bedford Army/Navy**
15 Bedford Park Blvd.
Bronx, NY 10468
(212) 367-0282

**Bell Army & Navy**
40-08 Bell Blvd.
Bayside, NY 11361
(718) 224-5098

**Bell Army & Navy**
46 West Montauk Hwy.
Lindenhurst, NY 11757
(516) 957-4363

**Bronx Sportsman**
2121 White Plains Rd.
Bronx, NY 10462
(212) 892-0520

**Brooklyn War Zone**
1108 39th St.
Brooklyn, NY 11218
(718) 854-5016

**Capital District Paintball**
Albany, NY
(518) 434-3621

**CIA Paintball**
945 Coney Island Ave.
Brooklyn, NY 11230
(718) 462-9731

**Cousins Army Navy**
19 Udall Rd.
West Islip, NY 11795
(516) 661-7419

**Fireball Mountain**
Friendship, NY
(716) 973-2817

**Forest Strategy Games**
Schaghticoke, NY
(518) 664-5851

**Indoor Splatball**
Buffalo, NY
(716) 383-5662

**Island Paintball**
905 East Jericho Tpk.

Huntington, NY 11746
(516) 692-7668

**JT's Paintball Zone, Inc.**
Rock Stream,NY
(607) 535-7285

**Liberty Paintball
Game, Ltd.**
Liberty, NY
(914) 292-7500

**Lyon's Den
Paintball Games**
Westfield, NY
(716) 326-6382

**Mad Mac's**
Mahopac, NY
(914) 628-3488

**Orion House**
1807 Cold Spring Rd.
Liverpool, NY 13090
(315) 451—0760

**Outback Sports**
150 Engineers Dr.
Hicksville, NY 11801
(516) 433-1010

**Outdoor Splatball**
Rochester, NY

(716) 383-5662

**Paintball Adventures**
10865 Wilson Road
Wolcott, NY 14590
(315) 587-4995

**Paintball Game Supplies**
160 Dispatch Drive
E. Rocherster, NY 14445
(716) 383-5662

**Paintball Park**
Constantia, NY
(315) 623-9067

**Paintball Survival
Game HQ**
945 Coney Island Ave.
Brooklyn, NY 11230
(718) 462-9731

**Paintball Unlimited**
1500 Military Rd.
Tonawanda,NY 14217
(716) 876-BALL

**Palenville Paintball Games**
Route 23A
Palenville, NY 12463
(800) 362-9695

**Porcupine Paintball**

86 E. 208 Street
Bronx, NY 10467
(212) 653-1691

**Precision Paintball**
2079A W. 6th St.
Brooklyn, NY 11223
(718) 714-0575

**Recon Challenge**
390 Columbia Tpk.
Rensselaer, NY 12144
(518) 477-7156

**Sudden Impact**
Bronx, NY
(212) 792-9044

**Survival New York**
295 Main Street
Mt. Kisco, NY 10549
(914) 241-0020

**Survivaly New York**
Sunset Camp Road
Plattekill, NY
(914) 241-0020

**Walt's Hobby Shop**
7909 Fifth Ave.
Brooklyn, NY 11209
(718) 745-4991

**Warriors World**
Albany, NY
(518) 437-0917

*Ohio*

**Action Enterpirses**
1014 Raab Road
Swanton, OH 43558
(419) 826-0744

**Blackhawk Park**
Route 1, Box 49C
Strasburg, OH 44680
(216) 878-7262

**Central Ohio Paintball**
800 Busch Court
Columbus, OH 43229
(614) 846-1104

**Combat Adventures**
295 South Second
Middleport, OH 45760
(614) 388-8601

**Combat Zone**
7060 S. TWP Rd. 131
Tiffin, OH 44883
(419) 447-8424

**Com-Sport Enterprises**

100 S. Edgehill Dr.
Fredericktown, OH 43019
(614) 694-1291

**Deer Run Paintball**
17124 Harmon-Patrick Rd.
Richwood, OH 43344

**Indian Springs Paintball**
2849 Summit Rd.
Akron, OH 44321
(216) 836-5106

**JONT Enterprises**
1396 New Garden Rd.
New Paris, OH 45347
(513) 437-7195

**Miami Valley Shooting**
7771 S. Cassel Rd.
Vandalia, OH 45377
(513) 890-1291

**Paintball Elite**
1090 Frank Rd #5
Columbus, OH 43223
(614) 274-7373

**Paintball Field of Fun**
Columbus, OH
(614) 846-1104

**Paintball Games Coliseum**

3621 State Route 273
Belle Center, OH 43310
(513) 464-4480

**Pinnacle Woods**
8752 East Ave.
Mentor, OH 44060
(216) 974-0077

**Splat Inc.**
3081 Dryden Rd.
Moraine, OH 45439
(513) 293-5560

**S. B.'s Paintball**
739 High Street
Lancaster, OH 43130
(614) 653-0638

**Splatland Paintball**
Wrightway Road N
Dayton, OH
(513) 293-5560

**Storm Paintball 638**
Reigert Square
Fairfield, OH 45014
(513) 887-1105

**Worlord's Paintball
Forest**
12133 Mayfield Rd.
Chardon. OH 44024

(216) 291-1802

## Pennsylvania

**Adventure World**
New Milford, PA
(717) 465-7007

**Cobra Command Inc**
41 Windsor Ct.
Lansdale, PA 19446
(215) 855-7398

**Cobra Command Store**
20 N. Cannon Ave.
Lansdale, PA 19446

**Combat Survival Games**
Littel Gap, PA
(215) 253-2211

**The Encounter**
515 Main St.
Stroudsburg, PA 18360
(717) 424-6132

**Frontline**
4369 Sunset Pike
Chambersburg, PA 17201
(717) 263-3700

**Foxhole, The**

Halifax, PA
(717) 362-8644

**Global War Zone**
Alburtis, PA
(215) 966-4780

**Highland Paintball**
Gaines, PA
(814) 435-1197

**Iron Triangle
Paintball Club**
7720 Chestnut St.
Zionville, PA 18092
(215) 965-4382

**Kuba's Surplus Sales**
231 W. 7th St.
Allentown, PA 18102
(215) 433-3877

**Operation Paintball**
Bridgeville, PA
(412) 221-0334

**Orion Paintball Sports**
Indiana, PA
(412) 349-8987

**Paintball Wizard**
2903 Bloom Rd.
Danville, PA 17821

(717) 275-5984

**Poco Loco**
Pottsdown, PA
(800) PLA-POCO

**Pro-Am Paintball**
20411 Terry Highway
Cranberry, PA 16033
(412) 776-3877

**Roman's Army Store**
4369 Sunset Pike
Chambersburg, PA 17201
(717) 761-3700

**Splatter at Jack Frost Mt.**
White Haven, PA
(800) 468-2442

**Sgt. York's**
900 Market St.
Lemoyne, PA 17043
(717) 761-3819

**Skirmish**
Jim Thrope, PA
(717) 325-3654

**Splatterdome**
Box 101
Southeastern, PA 19399
(215) 630-6767

**Three Rivers
Survival Game**
251 Westvue Rd.
Wexford, PA 15090
(412) 935-6100

**Urban Assault**
Pittsburg, PA
(412) 331-1080

## Wisconsin

**Paintball Dave's**
203 North Broadway
Milwaukee, WI 53202
(414) 271-3004

**Paintball Sam's**
Highway K
Racine, WI 53185
(414) 534-3197

**Paintball Games USA**
LaCrosse, WI
(414) 781-2784

**Splatterhouse Five**
Wausau, WI
(715) 573-0133

**Stalker Paintball Games**
N 1497 Southern Rd.
Lyndon Sta., WI

(608) 666-2400

**S.P.L.A.T. Camp**
Whitewater, WI
(414) 271-3004

**TNT Action Sports**
1011 19th St.
Monroe, WI 53566
(608) 325-3133

# Books and Magazines

Weekend Adventure Paintball, ($24.95). How to get started, where to play and strategy tips for beginners and experts.

A number of videos including: Wining Game; Paintball Pursuit; and SMG-60 Maintenance are available from I & I Sports, (310) 715-6800.

Other books available from many shops include: Official Survival Game Manual; Survival Game, tactics; Paintball Players Handbook, and others.

Action Pursuit Games Magazine, ($2.95 per issue, $24.50 annual subscription). Subscription Dept., P.O. Box 404, Mt. Morris, IL 61054 or (800) 877-5528

Paintball Sports Magazine, ($24.75 a year for the monthly publication). 540 Main St., Mt. Kisco, NY 10549.

Paintball News, (tabloid, 50-cents). P.O. Box 1608, 24 Henniler St., Hillsboro, NH 03244, (603) 464-6080.

# CHAPTER 8
# Paragliding

At first glance, paragliders resemble anorexic parachutes, but they have several unique design elements that enhance forward soaring performance, making them more maneuverable. Paragliders actually share many aerodynamic principals with an ordinary airplane wing. The high-tech design of the fabric overhead wing offers beginners almost instant gratification because the overall learning curve is quite short. The average person will be in the air and floating in almost no time.

"On balance, paragliding is the easiest and fastest aerial sport to learn. It's a terrific sport for anyone that is too busy, or doesn't have the upper body strength needed for the heavier hang glider, or who doesn't want to spend large sums of money to enjoy the airborne fun," says Bill Fifer, one of the few certified paraglider instructors in the Great Lakes region. "Because paragliding is less expensive than hang gliding and we can safely teach novices to fly off moderate hills in a long weekend, I see more and more paragliding coming to the Great Lakes states." Fifer also says the compact size and light weight of the equipment makes it very easy to travel with, and affordable.

Paragliding American-style is truly the new wave of flying. Weighing only 15-25 pounds, sport-level gear costs about $2,500. Thrill seekers living in the Great Lakes states can share that uplifting feeling with thousands of Europeans who pioneered the sport. You'll get a big thrill as the 250-square-foot nylon wing rises up behind you, filling with air and hauling you skyward at a smooth, slow pace over lush natural areas and along streams and rivers.

## Going aloft

Typically a neophyte paraglider can obtain their basic pilot's rating in 5-8 days (depending on weather conditions), for about $600, considerably less expensive and more quickly than hang glider students.

But, what is a paraglider, this banana-like aerial windbag that purports to be a cross between a hang glider a parachute? As I already mentioned, a paraglider is not a ram air parachute (a canopy with cells that fill with air and add lift and control), yet it's clear they are closely related. And the paraglider certainly owes its evolutionary history to the parachute. The modern, high-tech paraglider is computer designed and built from durable Dacron cloth and either kevlar or spectra lines that stretch very little as they secure you and the harness to the wing edges.

Your first flight, according to Fifer, will begin with your feet firmly patting across the ground. "Your first task is learning to manage and deploy the canopy behind you by facing into the wind. You'll flap about a little, thinking you'll tangle lines, but the teacher will be next to you offering instruction on how to check your forward and rear risers (canopy lines), and lifting them overhead as you run down a gentle slop."

To me at first, it resembled a tug-of-war with the winds using thin lines and a wide bed sheet, yet after only a few seconds the canopy takes shape as it scoops up the air. If you can

> *"To me at first, it resembled a tug-of-war with the winds using thin lines and a wide bed sheet..."*

keep running and keep the canopy centered overhead, the lift-filled wing will launch you into the air with a kick.

Beginning paragliding students are considered a candidate for a Class 1 pilot rating and you should seek an instructor with the following minimum qualifications: 1) an APA/USGHA Class 2 Pilot Rating; 2) an APA/USHGA Instructor Rating; and 3) experience.

## Paraglider control

Steering a paraglider in flight is similar to controlling a sky-diving parachute, a highly maneuverable canopy. Paragliders have two control lines, called brakes or steering lines, that extend from your hands to fan out to the trailing edge of each side of the wing. When you pull down on one of these brake lines the trailing edge angles down exactly like the flaps on an airplane. With the "flap" down you create drag on one side and the canopy will gently turn toward that side.

To descend or to ultimately land, the intrepid pilot merely

*First lessons along the beaches of Lake Michigan.*

pulls on both brake lines (toggles), stalling the canopy just as he contacts the ground. Advanced pilots can do flat turns, spin turns, "horseshoe collapsing" and other maneuvers, but paragliders fly slower than hang gliders.

Once you've learned the basic controls and taken enough lessons, you can quickly begin launches from taller hills or tows.

When you become experienced at finding thermals, which are columns of rising air, it's easy to paraglide over considerable distances, staying in the air for an hour or more. Because paragliders can make tight spirals in the air, you can ride thermals better than any other sport craft.

# Paragliding Services

As paragliding grows in popularity in the Great Lakes more and more hang glider operators/instructors will be offering training for paragliders pilots.

## *Michigan*

**Traverse City Hang Gliding/Paragliding**
Bill Fifer
1509 E. 8th Street
Traverse City, MI 49684
(616) 922-2844

## *New York*

**GMI**
Paragliding School
(516) 676-7599

# Other schools outside the Great Lakes Region

**Thermax Paragliding**
1500 E. Cedar #10
Flagstaff, AZ 86004
(602) 526-4579

**Glidell Skytime Paragliding**
555 Bryant St. Suite 256
Palo Alto, CA 94301
(415) 868-2413

## Accelerated Flight Systems
P.O. Box 1226
Del Mar, CA 92014
(619) 481-7400

## Rocky Mountain Paragliding
Box 2662 Canmore
Alberta, Canada TOLOMO
(403) 678-4973

## Alpine World's Adventure
5311 Western Ave
Boulder, CO 80301
(303) 440-0803

## Aspen Paragliding
417 S. Spring St.
Aspen, CO 81611
(303) COLORADO

## Fly America
P.O. Box 188
Shasta, CA 95087
(916) 359-2392

## Sun Valley Paragliding
P.O. Box 5715 301 Bell Dr.
Ketchum, ID 83340
(208) 726-3332

## Oregon Paragliding Assoc.
1012 NW Wall St.
Bend, OR 97701

(503) 389-5411

**Above & Beyond**
3314 W. 11400 S.
So. Jordan UT 84095
(801) 254-7455

For vacation-time thrill seekers, both novice and advanced, a number of paragliding holiday operators offer 3-7 day package tours near the Midwest.

Gliding Flight, a Utah-based tour operator, features terrific adventure tours, (801) 254-7455; Parapente USA offers 5-day tours in Idaho's Lemhi mountain range, (602) 292-1136; and, Fly the Sierra Nevada with Adventure Sports, (702) 883-7070.

## Equipment evolution

...*launching
pilots
off a flatbed
truck
is on
the increase...*

Paragliding began many years ago in the mountainous reaches of Europe where wild-eyed climbers invented a quicker way back down off the mountain. For many climbers in the Alps it simply wasn't enough to reach the summit safe and sound, you were also challenged to fly with the eagles off the mountain, catching invisible thermals and skimming the slopes back to the base camp. We won't be doing much of that in the Great Lakes, but we do benefit from the designing and refinement they made to the nylon wings.

Today's designs are sophisticated and practical, with top and bottom surface of thin Dacron held together by airfoil shaped panels (ribs) that separate the wing into as many as 24 gores or cells. Many of the cells are open in the front so the large canopy stays inflated with air from internal and dynamic pressure. Each of the high-strength lines are carefully placed along the glider's under-surface and extend to the harness. The lines are skillfully placed to insure the integrity of the airfoil shape, allowing a good angle of attack and anhedral. The curve of the wing when inflated with air is crescent-shaped and is necessary to create outward forces at the tips that keep the wind from flapping inward. Stabilizers at the tip hang down to assist in yaw or side to side stability.

## Buying your first paraglider

"Typical sport paragliders are about 30 feet from tip to tip.

*Lift and thermals are great in the winter.*

Beginner or Class 1 canopies usually have a wider root cord (front to back) and are much more stable," says Fifer, a dealer of many models of paragliders. "Buying a quality paraglider, suited for your own skill level is an important step. First-time buyers should consult their instructor, who knows your capabilities and is likely a dealer, which is actually a great service for the new pilot."

Class 1 canopies are more stable and forgiving of beginners. If you are a beginner buy only a level 1 canopy, and only upgrade to Class 2 or 3, which have slippery performance characteristics for advanced pilots only. Class 2 canopies fly faster and soar better when guided by an expert who can handle collapses, which these models are prone to have. This type of high-life canopy requires expert piloting, though it also boasts lower sink rates and higher flight speeds. These performance characteristics allow for infinitely better rides, permitting longer, higher flights, and great fun riding the thermals.

Many enthusiasts believe towing (launching pilots off a flatbed truck) is on the increase, so determine what type of flying you will be doing, and research and test fly the canopy before you buy. Also check the harness and any UV damage from the sun on lines and fabric.

## Books and Magazines

Paragliding — the Magazine, ($26, annual). P.O. Box 477, Riverton, Utah 84065, (801) 254-7455. Voice of the American Paragliding Association (APA).

Paragliding USA (magazine) Performance Designs, 12650 Softwind Drive, Moreno, CA 92389.

Paragliding Flight, by Dennis Pagen, ($19.95), is 208 pages of instruction. Sport Aviation Publications, P.O. Box 101, Mingoville, PA 16856.

Understanding the Sky, by Dennis Pagen, ($19.95), is 288 pages, with 270 photos and illustrations, plus a complete weather guide. Also from Sport Aviation Publications.

Paragliding — A Pilot's Training Manual, by Wills Wing, ($19.95), is 140 pages with 62 illustrations on skills, aerodynamics, weather equipment, and more. From Wills Wing, 500 Blueridge Ave., Orange, CA 92665.

Touching Cloudbase, by Ian Currer and Rob Cruickshank, ($18), has 20 color photos and 45 illustrations that cover all aspects of flying. From Touching Cloudbase, 3314 W. 11400 South, South Jordan, UT 84065.

Paragliding in America, by Marcus Salvemini, ($12), lists 40 major U.S. flying sites in 120 pages. From Airtek Paragliding, (619) 454-0598.

Cross County (magazine), 752 Casiano Drive #B, Santa Barbara, CA 93105, (805) 687-4663 or fax (805) 968-0059.

Skywings (magazine), 73 Upper Harlestone, Northhampton NN7 4E, England. Phone: 44-604-587.

ABC of Paragliding, by Hubert Aupetit, Vol. Libre Diffusion, 3 rue Ampere, F-94200 Ivry, France.

Walking on Air — Paragliding, by Dennis Pagen, Rd. 2, Box 355P, Bellefonte, PA 16823, (814) 383-2569.

An Introduction to Paragliding, by Zygmunt Frankel, 4 Nathan Street, Ramat-Gan 52450, Israel.

## Video

Parasol World Championships, ($49.95), is 55 minutes of the 1991 championships in France.

Thermik — The Art of Flying, ($49.95), is 40 minutes of the basics featuring all aspects of paragliding and hang gliding. Meteorology is covered. Adventure Video, 4750 Townsite Road, Reno, NV 89511, (702) 849-9672.

CHAPTER 9

# Scuba diving

## Taking the Plunge

The weightless world under the surface of the Great Lakes is unlike anything above the surface. Scuba diving takes you to a new world, of unfounded freedom, unbounded gravity and an underwater realm of life and scenery rarely seen, rarely understood. The Great Lakes' thousands of miles of diving opportunity provides an endless resource for recreation, learning, discovery, and thrills.

One of the most popular introductions to the underwater world is snorkeling. Using a mask, fins and snorkel to gently wander about shallow waters is easy to learn for all ages, and is a perfect family activity. After a few hours snorkeling, learning to use a mask and fins, many thrill seekers are ready to begin training for their first scuba dive.

## Getting started

Learning to scuba dive is often referred to as "getting certified." The process of learning to safely dive is a combination of classroom study, pool practice, and supervised open water lessons and practice. Introductory classes are often offered at your local diving store or YMCA, even community education programs often offer quality instruction at a nominal fee.

PADI or NAUI (National Association of Underwater Instructors) are the most widely recognized, so select a PADI or NAUI training facility if possible. These instructors usually keep class size small, stress individualized instruction, and offer lots of practice time.

When looking for a quality diving school ask the following questions: How much does the course cost, including open water dives? How many hours are spent in the pool vs. open water? Is the training pool deep enough to permit proper equalization? (Many instructors prefer pools that are 10 feet deep.) What dive equipment are you asked to buy? Are there package deals that include quality equipment and lessons for one lower price? How long has the facility been in business, how many pupils have it certified, and how long has the instructor been teaching? Also ask how many students will be in each class? Can you get a refund if you don't pass certification, or can you purchase extra days of instruction one at a time? Where, when and how are the open water sessions offered? Quality facilities will give reassuring answers to these and other questions.

## Classroom

When you think of thrill sports, even the most crazed devotees began their wild careers in a dusty classroom, filling their noggins with textbook stuff. Today, a large part of the textbook material is provided in easy-to-understand work sheets, videos and personal instructions. The training covers the theory of diving, physiology, the marine environment, safety, practical issues about equipment costs and maintenance, and environmental issues.

## Pool session

After a few hours of dry classroom instruction, you'll be ready for the real thing, albeit in the safe calm waters of a swimming pool. Here's where equipment and its use and maintenance is introduced, and attempted under the guidance of an instructor in the warm pool. Pool sessions build confidence and soon students feel comfortable with the awkward equipment and hiss of the regulators. A brief skills test is required both in the pool and in open water. Before certification you'll also be required to pass a written test.

> *Pool sessions build confidence*

## Open water

Great Lakes area scuba divers have many options for open water lessons. From warm inland lakes, even small ponds, to the emerald freshwater that surrounds us from Lake Erie and Ontario to the cold waters of Lake Superior.

Open water sessions are the final phase in your training and where your pool work and classroom skills come together under the supervision of an instructor. Some operators offer diving from docks, while most have dive boats where the class may spend an entire day or weekend gaining experience.

## How long does it take?

The traditional course, unlike the resort-based or vacation certification varieties, requires about six classroom sessions, six pool sessions, and four open water outings.

Personalized instruction is also often offered at dive shops, where busy students can customize their course and class schedule.

## What does it cost?

The basic certification course can cost $200 to $300, depending on open water diving costs. Some courses include all equipment and all dives, while others only offer equipment for pool sessions, and so on. Exotic open water destinations will, of course, cost more. Ask about costs up front, get complete details, and try to meet and spend some time with the instructor.

Equipment, as with most sports, can be expensive if you become serious. But plan on spending about $1,200 to $1,500 for safe basic equipment: a vest, tanks, regulator, fins, mask, calculator, watch, and gauge.

## Shops, lessons, resources centers

### *Illinois*

**Adventures in Scuba**
1730 West Fullerton
Chicago, IL

(312) 935-3483

**Adventures Underwater**
1400 South 5th St.
Springfield, IL
(217) 753-3355

**Aqua Diving School**
134 North Detroit St.
Morton, IL
(309) 263-0045

**Barracuda Brad's
Dive Shop**
680 South Eastwood Dr.
Woodstock, IL
(815) 337-2822

**Berry's Scuba**
6674 Northwest Highway
Chicago, IL
(312) 763-1626

**Dive Systems Inc.**
1812 Taft Ave.
Berkeley, IL
(708) 449-3467

**Diventures Inc.**
1017 West Diverscy
Chicago, IL
(312) 348-3483

**Do Dive**
81.11 North university
Peoria, IL
(309) 692-7600

**Elite Diving & Rec.
Activities**
340 West Cherry
Winchester, IL
(217) 742-3241

**Forest City Scuba**
1894 Daimier Rd.
Rockford, IL
(815) 398-7119

**Frogg Pond Dive Shop**
2310 Skoke Valley Rd.
Highland Park, IL
(708) 432-5055

**Goose's Scuba Shack**
18143 Torrence Ave.
Lansing, IL
(708) 474-7380

**Great Lakes Divers**
541 South La Grange Rd.
La Grange, IL
(708) 482-7788

**Illinois Institute of Diving**
436 Roosevelt Rd.

Glen Ellyn, IL
(708) 858-4485

**Lake Michigan Scuba Inc.**
400 East Rand Rd.
Lake Zurich, IL
(708) 540-7211

**Loves Park Scuba**
7307 North Alpine
Loves Park, IL
(815) 633-6969

**Mid America Scuba II**
5900 North Illinois, Suite 9
Fairview Heights, IL
(618) 624-8881

**Midwest Diving Specialist**
203 South Linden
Normal, IL
(309) 452-0222

**Midwest Scuba Center**
700 South Neil St.
Campaign, IL
(217) 352-3118

**Peoria Dive Center Inc.**
1605 Tremont St.
East Peoria, IL
(309) 822-8388

**Prospect Dive &
Sport Center**
870 South Arthur
Arlington, IL
(708) 259-0606

**Scuba Diving School
of America**
4 South 100 Rt. 59 Unit 19
Naperville, IL
(708) 393-9410

**Scuba Emporium**
12003 South Ciero
Alsip, IL
(708) 389-9410

**Scuba Systems Ltd.**
3919 Oakton St.
Skokie, IL
(708) 674-0222

**Sea Level Dive Shop**
1809 South Route 31
Mchenry, IL
(815) 344-9732

**Sentry Pool Inc.**
1529 46th Ave.
Moline, IL
(309) 797-9721

**T. L. Fritts Co.**

527 Davis St.
Evanston, IL
(708) 446-6694

**The Ocean's Door**
225 East Deerpath Rd.
Lake Forest, IL
(708) 295-0787

**Undersea Scuba Center**
611 North Addison Rd.
Villa Park, IL
(708) 833-8383

**Underwater Safaris**
620 North La Salle St.
Chicago, IL
(312) 337-7730

**Venture Forth Scuba**
2424 South Alpine
Rockford, IL
(815) 229-5658

**West Shore Aquasports**
1201 Sheridan Rd.
Winthrop Harbor, IL
(708) 872-9791

**Windwalker Scuba**
4624 North Illinois
Bellville, IL
(618) 233-0643

## *Indiana*

**Anchor Dive Shop**
1720 Lake Ave.
Fort Wayne, IN
(219) 426-3493

**Big Red Divers Supply Inc.**
820 West 17th St. Suite 14
Bloomington, IN
(812) 331-1110

**Deep Desires Scuba**
916 East Main Suite 200
Muncie, IN
(317) 786-8030

**Divers Supply Muncie**
3715 South Walnut
Muncie, IN
(317) 288-4868

**Divers Supply Co.**
1079 Broadripple Rd.
Indianapolis, IN
(317) 253-2000

**Divers World**
1271 East Morgan
Evansville, IN
(812) 432-2738

**Diving Den Inc.**

2229 East OO N.S.
Kokomo, IN
(317) 452-1034

**DNP Diving**
604 East Main
Logansport, IN
(219) 735-3483

**Evansville Scuba
Center Inc.**
1319 North First Ave.
Evansville, IN
(812) 424-6667

**Lake County Divers**
305 Main St, Rt. 51
Hobart, IN

(219) 942-0016

**Mermaid Quest**
305 East McKinley Ave.
Mishawaka, IN
(219) 256-6875

**Michigan City
Scuba Center**
510 East Second St.
Michigan City, IN
(219) 874-0058

**Midwest Scuba Center**
4306 West 96th St.
Indianapolis, IN
(317) 872-2522
**Pro Dive Shop**

3203 Covington Rd.
Ft. Wayne, IN
(219) 432-7745

**Scuba Adventures**
1079 Broad Ripple Ave.
Indianapolis, IN
(317) 253-2000

**Seaweed Divers**
1121 State St.
New Albany, IN
(812) 949-8060

**Southern Indiana Scuba**
1023 South walnut
Bloomington, IN
(812) 336-2527

**The Scuba Tank**
105 Library Lane
Valparaiso, IN
(219) 477-4454

## Michigan

**A & C Diving**
4280 Plainfield Ave. NE
Grand Rapids, MI
(616) 363-7711

**Advance Aquatics, Inc.**
25020 East Jefferson

St. Clair Shores, MI
(313) 779-8777

**Adventure Sports**
1100 Bay View Rd.
Petosky, MI
(616) 347-3041

**Brunos Dive Shop**
34740 Gratiot
Mt. Clemens, MI
(616) 792-2040

**Deep Six Scuba Schools**
884 Pine Rd.
Essexville, MI
(517) 892-2715

**Dive Site**
9125 Portage Rd.
Kalamazoo, MI
(616) 323-3700

**Divers Down Scuba Shop**
717 3rd St.
Marquette, MI
(906) 225-1699

**Divers Inc.**
42295 Ann Arbor Rd.
Plymouth, MI
(313) 451-5430

**Divers Inc.**
3380 Washtenaw Ave.
Ann Arbor, MI
(313) 971-7770

**Diver's Mast**
2900 Lansing Ave.
Jackson, MI
(517) 784-5862

**Don's Dive Shop**
29480 West Ten Mile
Farmington, MI
(313) 477-7333

**Great Lakes Dive**
Locker Inc.
4909 South Division
Wyoming, MI
(616) 531-9440

**Great Lakes Scuba**
2187 North US 31 South
Traverse City, MI
(616) 946-1602

**Lake Orion Divers Den**
604 South Lapeer Rd.
lake Orion, MI
(517) 867-4527

**M & M Diving**
1901 10th St.

Menominee, MI
(906) 863-7330

**Macomb Dive Center**
13465 East 12 Mile Rd.
Warren, MI
(313) 558-9922

**Michigan Underwater
School of Diving**
3820 Fort St.
Lincoln Park, MI
(313) 388-1322

**Ocean Sands Scuba**
780 South Columbia Ave.
Holland, MI
(616) 396-0068

**Recreational Diving
Systems**
4424 North Woodward
Royal Oak, MI
(313) 549-0303

**Scuba North**
13380 West Bayshore Dr.
Traverse City, MI
(616) 947-2520

**Seaquatics**
5027 Eastman Rd.
Midland, MI

(517) 835-6391

**Seaside Diving**
28612 Harper
St. Clair Shores, MI
(313) 772-3581

**Skamt Scuba Shop Inc.**
5055 Plainfield Ave. NE
Grand Rapids, MI
(616) 364-9880

**St. Clair Scuba
Training Center**
8655 Dixie Hwy.
Fair Haven, MI
(313) 725-1991

**Sub Aquatics Sport**
347 North Helmer St.
Battle Creek, MI
(616) 968-8551

**Summit Sports**
224 East Chisolm
Alpena, MI
(517) 835-6391

**The Dive Shop Inc.**
G 4020 Corunna Rd.
Flint, MI
(313) 732-3900

**The Scuba Shack**
P.O. Box 213
Higgins Lake, MI
(517) 821-6477

**Tom & Jerry's Scuba**
20318 Van Born Rd.
Dearborn Heights, MI
(313) 278-1124

**Underwater Outfitters**
2579 Union Lake Rd.
Commerce Township, MI
(313) 363-2224

**US Scuba Center**
3260 South Rochester Rd.
Rochester, MI
(313) 853-2800

**Wolf's Divers Supply**
250 West Main St.
Benton Harbor, MI
(616) 926-1068

**ZZ Underwater
World, Inc.**
1806 East Michigan Ave.
Lansing, MI
(517) 485-3894

## *New York*

**All American Sport Shops**
27 North Broad St.
Norwich, NY
(607) 334-5277

**Aqua Dive Inc.**
951 Jewett Ave.
Staten Island, NY
(718) 442-0023

**Aquatic Center of Rochester**
2199 East Henrietta Rd.
Rochester, NY
(716) 334-1670

**Aquatic World of North Syracuse**
114 Kreischer Rd.
N. Syracuse, NY
(315) 458-1955

**Atlantic Divers Ltd.**
501 Kings hwy.
Brooklyn, NY
(718) 625-4582

**Byram Bay Sports Inc.**
500 North Main St.,
2nd Floor
Port Chester, NY
(914) 937-2685

**Capt. Mike's Diving Center**
634 City Island Ave.
Bronx, NY
(212) 885-1588

**Cougar Sports**
917 Saw Mill River Rd.
Ardsley, NY
(914) 693-8877

**Crandall's Scuba**
1590 1/2 Pennsylvania Ave.
Pine City, NY
(607) 733-6901

**Danny's Dive Shop**
2150 Grand Ave.
Baldwin, NY
(516) 223-8989

**Dip N' Dive**
500 Niagara Falls Blvd.
Buffalo, NY
(716) 837-3483

**Dive Inc.**
1 south Central Ave.
Valley Stream, NY
(516) 872-4571

**Dive Locker**
621 East Boston

Mamaroneck, NY
(914) 381-5935

**Divers' Rendez-Vous**
79-07 Grand Ave.
Elmhurst, NY
(718) 478-4097

**Divers Way**
596 Sunrise Hwy.
Bayshore, NY
(516) 665-7990

**Divers World**
1383 Vischer Ferry Rd.
Clifton Park, NY
(518) 373-0521

**Divers Discovery**
1629 Central Ave.
Albany, NY
(518) 456-8146

**Dolphin Divers Inc.**
250-14 northern Blvd.
Little Neck, NY
(718) 667-3232

**Dutchess Diving Center**
503 South Rd. Rt. 9
Poughkeepsie, NY
(914) 462-0255

**East Coast Diving Inc.**
1500 Hyland Blvd.
Staten Island, NY
(718) 979-6056

**Fantasea Ski/Sports Inc.**
2519 Hylan Blvd.
Staten Island, NY
(718) 667-3232

**Harvey's Dive Center**
3179 Emmons Ave.
At Sheepheads Bay
Brooklyn, NY
(718) 743-0055

**Hudson River Scuba Sales**
Route 44
Pleasant, Valley, NY
(914) 635-3488

**Hunt Underwater
Specialist**
Box 832
Watertown, NY
(315) 788-2075

**Innerspace Dive Shop**
57 Forest Ave.
Glen Cove, NY
(516) 671-5454

**Island Scuba Center**

74 Woodcleft Ave.
Freeport, NY
(516) 546-2030

**King's Country Divers**
2417 Ave. U
Brooklyn, NY
(718) 648-4232

**Marsh Scuba Supply**
19 Lauer Rd.
Poughkeepsie, NY
(914) 452-8994

**Marshall's Pro Diving Svc.**
5051 North Frontenac Rd.
Trumanburg, NY
(607) 387-7321

**Martini Scuba Inc.**
2037 Central Park Ave.
Yonkers, NY
(914) 779-7361

**Mel's Dive Shop**
91 Miller St.
Plattsburg, NY
(518) 561-7138

**Middletown Scuba**
Rt. 17 Dolson Ave.
Middletown, NY
(914) 343-2858

**National Aquatics Service**
1732 Erie Blvd. East
Syracuse, NY
(315) 479-5544

**Ontario Scuba**
170 West First St. South
Fulton, NY
(315) 593-8040

**Pan Aqua Diving Inc.**
101 West 75th St.
New York, NY
(212) 496-2267

**Paragon Sporting Goods**
101 East 18th St.
New York, NY
(212) 255-8036

**Peconic Scuba**
1140 Flanders Rd.
Riverhead, NY
(516) 727-7578

**Point Breeze Dive Shop**
9456 Lake Shore Rd.
Angola, NY
(716) 549-3766

**Port Jefferson Diver**
811 Route 25A
Pt. Jefferson, NY

(516) 331-9609

**Professional Scuba Center**
5777 Camp Road
Hamburg, NY
(716) 648-3483

**Richard's Sporting Goods**
233 West 42nd St.
New York, NY
(800) 783-3483

**Regional Rivers**
328 North Plank Rd.
Newburgh, NY
(914) 566-1122

**S-54 Divers Corporation**
341 Central Ave.
Scarsdale, NY
(914) 472-3104

**Scuba Hut Inc.**
141 West Commercial St.
East Rochester, NY
(716) 385-6430

**Scuba Network**
290 Atlantic
Brooklyn, NY
(718) 802-0700

**Scuba Network**

116 East 57th St.
New York, NY
(212) 750-9160

**Scuba Network**
Headquarters Plaza
Morristown, NY
(201) 539-2424

**Scuba Network**
175 5th Ave.
New York, NY
(212) 228-2080

**Scuba Network**
341 Central Park
Scarsdale, NY
(914) 472-3104

**Scuba Network**
271 Walt Witman Rd.
Rte.110
Huntington Stat., NY
(516) 673-2811

**Scuba Network**
245-C Old Country Rd.
Carle Place, NY
(516) 997-4864

**Scuba Training &
Equipment Center**
12 Bobby Lane

West Nyack, NY
(914) 358-6250

**Scuba University**
357 Milton Ave.
Balston Spa, NY
(518) 885-8554

**Seafan Scuba Center**
101 East Main St.
Endicott, NY
(607) 754-0873

**Sea Horse Divers**
95-58 Queens Blvd.
Rego Park, NY
(718) 897-2885

**Seascapes Dive Center**
737-A Smithtown Bypass
Smithtown, NY
(516) 366-4588

**Seascapes Dive Center Inc.**
317 Jackson Ave.
Syosset, NY
(516) 496-7833

**Staten Island Scuba**
and Snorkel Center
372 Cleveland Ave.
Staten Island, NY
(718) 966-6280

**Stingray Divers**
762 Grand St.
Brooklyn, NY
(718) 384-1280

**Suffolk Diving Center**
58 Larkfield Rd.
East Northport, NY
(516) 261-4388

**Swim King Dive Shop**
572 Route 25A
Rocky Point, NY
(516) 744-7707

**The Diving Center**
26 Wolcott Rd.
Levittown, NY
(516) 796-6560

**The Scuba Shoppe**
1870-C Rte. 112
Medford, NY
(516) 289-5555

**Tiedmann's Diving Center**
26 Wolcott Rd.
Levittown, NY
(516) 796-6560

**Underwater World Inc.**
3028 Merrick Rd.

Wantaugh NY
(516) 679-9709

**Under World Dive Shop**
P.O. Box 39
219 Main St.
Newfield, NY
(607) 654-3306

**U.S. Sports Dist. Inc.**
200 6th St.
Brooklyn, NY
(718) 802-0700

**Westchester Dive Inc.**
500 North Main St.
Port Chester, NY
(914) 937-2685

## *Ohio*

**Ask Water Sports**
6522 Riverside Drive
Dublin, OH
(614) 889-2822

**Adventures in Diving**
14397 Pearl Rd.
Strongville, OH
(216) 572-2005

**Anchor Dive Center of N Olmsted**
28669 Luralle Rd.
North Olmsted, OH
(216) 779-9660

**Aqua Hut International**
5030 Bennett
Toledo, OH
(419) 476-3100

**Aqua Specialists**
14813 Madison Ave.
Cleveland, OH
(216) 521-4855

**Aquanuts**
320 South State #G
Westerville, OH
(614) 891-1234

**Aquatic Center**
1080 1/2 Gleenwood Ave.
Napoleon, OH
(419) 592-9876

**B & K Diving Services**
154 Park Ave.
Mansfield, OH
(419) 524-3557

**Buckeye Diving School**
46 Warrensville Center
Bedford, OH
(216) 439-3677

**C & J Scuba Supply**
5825 North Dixie Hwy.

Dayton, OH
(513) 890-6900

**Central Ohio School
of Diving**
2355 West Dublin/
Granville Rd.
Columbus, OH
(614) 889-5678

**Cincinnati Diving Center**
8412 Winton Rd.
Cincinnati, OH
(513) 521-3483

**D & M Diving**
1473 Canton Rd.
Akron, OH
(216) 784-1414

**Dales Diving Shop Inc.**
302 Meigs St.
Sandusky, OH
(419) 625-4134

**Deep Six Specialists**
1074 Brown St.
Akron, OH
(216) 724-8737

**Divers Den**
7203 Beechmont Ave.
Cincinnati, OH

**Divers Paradise**
2511 North Reynolds
Toledo, OH
(419) 535-6828

**Divers' Port 'O' Call Inc.**
5418 Mayfield Rd.
Ludhurst, OH
(216) 473-4837

**Dive Inc.**
961 East Dublin-Granville
Columbus, OH
(614) 785-0950

**East Gate Scuba**
8358 Ohio Pike
Cincinnati, OH
(513) 752-7681

**Kapuka Wai Dive Shop**
1506 Whipple Ave. NW
Canton, OH
(216) 478-2511

**Miami Valley School
of Diving**
871 East Franklin Rd.
Centerville, OH
(513) 434-3483

**New Wave**
325 West Lake Shore Dr.

Port Clinton, OH
(419) 734-2240

**Ohio Divers Supply Inc.**
9612 Wollam Rd.
Bradner, OH
(419) 457-8765

**Scuba Adventures**
8088 Beechmont Ave.
Cincinnati, OH
(513) 474-9600

**Scuba Unlimited**
8966 Blue Ash Rd.
Cincinnati, OH
(513) 793-4747

**Sub-Aquatics Inc.**
8855 Broad St.
Reynolds, OH
(614) 864-1235

**The Underwater
Connections Inc.**
1607 West 5th Ave.
Columbus, OH
(614) 487-9777

**Treasure Cove Scuba**
1041 Youngstown
Niles, OH
(216) 544-6230

**Underwater Dive Inc.**
42551 North Ridge
Elyria, OH
(216) 324-3434

## Pennsylvania

**Adventure Sports**
1685 Lincoln Ways East
Chambersburg, PA
(717) 267-3604

**Anchor Line Scuba**
1032 North Providence Rd.
Media, PA
(215) 566-2330

**Aqua Hut**
4327 Main
Philadelphia, PA
(215) 483-8408

**Aquatic Adventures**
5992-B Steubenville Pike
McKees Rocks, PA
(412) 788-4511

**Bainbridge
Sportsmen's Club**
R.D. #1 Box 23-1
Bainsbridge, PA
(717) 426-2114

**B & B Marine Specialist**
Hillsville-Bessemer Rd.
P.O. Box 277
Hillsville, PA
(412) 667-9448

**Blue Fin Dive Shop**
239 Concord Rd.
Aston, PA
(215) 494-4787

**Deep 6 Dive Center Ltd.**
R. D. #1
Hesston, PA
(814) 658-3595

**Divers World**
1904 West 26th St.
Erie, PA
(814) 459-3195

**Doc's Diving Ltd.**
275 2nd St. Pike
Southampton, PA
(215) 364-0408

**Duda's Diving Duds**
101 Bartrams Lane
Westchester, PA
(215) 436-0176

**Fayette Scuba**
Rd. 1 Box 76

Vanderbilt, PA
(412) 529-2001

**Forgotten Fin Dive Shop**
3105 Perkiomen Ave.
Redding, PA
(215) 779-3488

**Harrisburg Scuba Center**
3997 Sunnycrest Dr.
Harrisburg, PA
(717) 561-0517

**Harrisburg Scuba Center**
2314 Fiddlers Elbow Rd.
Hummelstown, PA

**Jolly Roger Dive Shop**
198 Millardsville Rd.
Richland, PA
(717) 866-5535

**Main-Line Divers Inc.**
51 Rittenhouse Place
Ardmore, PA
(215) 642-3483

**Mid Atlantic Scuba**
3600 St. Road
Ben Salem, PA
(215) 245-0141

**Pittsburgh Scuba**

314 North Craig St.
Pittsburgh, PA
(412) 621-9900

**Professional Diving Service**
1135 Pittsburgh St.
Springdale, PA
(412) 274-7719

**Randy's Dive Shop**
#6 Sandy Hill Rd.
Irwin, PA
(412) 863-0752

**Scuba America**
1554 Gardner
Scranton, PA
(717) 342-1480

**Scuba Tank**
4102 Bath Pike
Bethlehem, PA
(215) 868-7373

**Scuba Venture Inc.**
124 Penn Hwy.
Sinking Spring, PA
(215) 678-2688

**Sea World Divers Inc.**
1820 Union Blvd.
Allentown, PA
(215) 432-6866

**Smiley's Scuba Shop Inc.**
12985 Perry Hwy.
Wexford, PA
(412) 935-6667

**Smokey's Divers Den**
412 North Duke St.
Lancaster, PA
(717) 393-5333

**Sunken Treasure
Dive Shop**
R.D. 4 Box 523C
Jersey Shore, PA
(717) 398-1458

**The Scuba Tank**
4102 Bath Pike
Bethlehem, PA
(215) 868-7373

**Underwater World**
495 Easton Rd.
Horsham, PA
(215) 672-4180

**Underwater World**
14 Morris Ave.
Bryn Mawr, PA
(215) 527-9681

**York Diver**
968 S. George St.

York, PA
(717) 846-0400

## Wisconsin

**Aqua Center**
628 Bellevue St.
Green Bay, WI
(414) 468-8080

**Bennett Academy of S & S**
6509 West North Ave.
Wauwatosa, WI
(414) 258-6440

**Central Wisconsin
Diving Academy**
8751 Hwy. 13 South
Wisconsin Rapids, WI
(715) 325-3888

**Dive Point Scuba**
632 Isadore
Stevens Point, WI
(715) 344-3483

**Dive USA**
134 West Main
Theinsville, WI
(414) 242-3483

**Divers Delight**
1322 North Main

West Bend, WI
(414) 334-6057

**Diving Unlimited**
130 West 2nd St.
Oconomowoc, WI
(414) 567-0802

**Erwin's Scuba Center**
5730 108th St.
Hales Corner, WI
(414) 425-6924

**Fontana Sports Specialists**
251 State St.
Madison, WI
(414) 275-2220

**Hi-Lo Scuba**
3249 West Greenfield
Milwaukee, WI
(414) 672-5035

**Inland Divers Supply**
411 Kimberly Dr.
Chippewa Falls, WI
(715) 723-9408

**Island Diving Inc.**
RR 2 Island Rd.
Hayer City, WI
(715) 792-2534

**Klein Scuba**
1414 West Campus
Wausau, WI
(715) 675-6722

**Lakeshore Scuba**
239 Pennsylvania Ave.
Sheboygan, WI
(414) 457-3483

**Marineland of Onalaska**
412 Campbell
Onalaska, WI
(608) 783-3186

**Mountain Bay
Ski and Dive**
200 Mall Dr.
Appleton, WI
(414) 731-3652

**Reefpoint Diving Center**
5600 Spring St.
Racine, WI
(414) 886-8501

**Winsor's Pro Diving**
Route 4 Box 4800
Hayward, WI
(715) 634-5122

**3 Little Devils Diving Shop**
Route 4 Hwy. 123

Baraboo, WI
(608) 356-5122

# Organizations

**International Diving Educators Associations**
P.O. Box 8427
Jacksonville, FL 32239-8427
(904) 744-5554

**National Association of Scuba Diving Schools**
8099 Indiana Avenue
Riverside, CA 92504
(909) 687-8792

**National Association of Underwater Instructors**
P.O. Box 14650
Montclair, CA 91763
(909) 621-5801

**PADI International**
1251 E. Dyer Rd. Suite 100
Santa Ana, CA 92705-5605
(714) 540-7234

**Professional Diving Instructors Corporation**
1015 River Street
Scranton, PA 18505
(717) 342-9434

**Scuba School International**
2619 Canton Court
Fort Collins, CO 80525

(303) 482-0883

**National YMCA Scuba Program Oakbrook Square**
6083-A Oakbrook Parkway
Norcross/Atlanta, GA 30093
(404) 662-5172

# Books and Magazines

Skin Diver Magazine, (monthly, $3.95), P.O. Box 51473, Boulder, CO 80323-1473.

Dive Michigan and Dive Wisconsin

CHAPTER 10

Skydiving

This is it, the ultimate thrill sport. Your heart simply can't beat any harder or any faster. Hurling yourself out of an aircraft with a tiny bag of nylon strapped to your back as your only protection against the really great beyond is truly a thrill.

"If you picture skydiving as a hapless, crazed daredevil blasting uncontrolled through the air, then dangling beneath a directionless canopy and finally slamming to a hard landing on harder ground...you're wrong," says Michigan skydiver Jerry Werle who took up the sport at the age of 54.

The fact is more than 115,000 skydivers annually make 2.4 million jumps with rarely an accident. These intrepid jumpers use modern, highly maneuverable main parachutes and other fancy equipment to enjoy the benefits of a very sophisticated and technical sport. Convinced yet?

While statistically, skydiving is a pretty safe activity (it does have it's routine injuries) many thrill seekers seem to draw the line at this ballistic sport. Seemingly, the statistic that one in

80,000 jumps ends in a fatality (usually human error) scares off even the hardy risk addicts. Nevertheless, you are actually safer skydiving than driving to work in some parts of the country. *Geronamo!*

> **"Real thrill seekers can take a first-time tandem jump or free fall in the secure grasp of skilled instuctors on their first day of training"**

"Unlike 70 years ago when skydivers began competing...today's jump schools and drop zones are safety driven. They teach standardized programs better and faster and offer the newest techniques, such as tandem jumping and accelerated free fall (AFF), where students can learn the sport in less time. Real thrill seekers can take a first-time tandem jump or free fall in the secure grasp of skilled instructors on their first day of the training," says Werle.

## How to Start

First, according to Werle, "find the best jump school in your area (see the listing). Because sport skydiving is carefully regulated by the U.S. Parachuting Association, most USPA jump schools are highly professional, offering the latest equipment, techniques, and the most experienced instructors."

Although skydiving training is increasingly standardized there are differences between schools, so choose a program carefully. The most important things to consider when shopping for an instructor and school is their safety record, overall quality of instruction, reliable aircraft, modern safe equipment, locations, and the cost and times of lessons and training sessions.

## Safety

"Schools and drop zones are required to log jumps and keep track of any injuries, even scrapes and twisted ankles," says Werle. Top jump schools will log thousands of training jumps without serious problems. As with searching for any training, look for long-established, full-time facilities with jump masters and instructors who have logged thousands of jumps and taught hundreds of students. Tandem and AFF instructors should have special training and USPA certification in those areas.

The bigger jump schools will operate twin engine aircraft that can take you higher faster, saving travel time and offering more free fall time. All should have well-maintained equipment and a serious, professional attitude toward safety and skills development.

## Training, then jumping

Training begins in the classroom. Whether your jump school offers the traditional static line or AFF program, you will spend about five hours absorbing the basic principles of the sport, including: safety in the air, in the aircraft, and on the ground after landing; equipment and rigging; emergency procedures; flying; and landing the canopy. You will view educational films or video tapes. The training may also include hanging a few feet off the ground in a parachute harness, practicing landing skills and getting the feel of the rigging.

When the ground training is completed, and when you are ready, you will have three types of jumps to choose from: traditional static line; tandem; or accelerated free fall. "For decades static line jumps were the standard in maiden training jumps.

But because it allows no free fall time, many drop zones are slowly phasing out the static line jumping and focusing their training on tandem and accelerated free fall. In fact, many schools are experimenting with all three types of jumps and melding training programs that use the best of each style," says Werle.

## Static line

Remember those paratroopers in the old war movies nervously snapping their static line hooks to a wire clothesline inside the shaking war bird? Then they jumped out — probably at low altitude — and the static line jerked the chute open, offering intrepid jumpers about a half-a-second of free fall before their neck was snapped by the opening round canopy. Well, it is not that way in modern skydiving training.

"Static line jumping is still preferred by many drop zones, and a single jump will cost about $150, that includes training, rental of equipment, and payment for the pilot and instruction and the aircraft," says Werle, "and, frankly, it is still worth-while for those jumpers who value a 'one-time' experience, or for serious students who are beginning their training."

Normally, after about five or six static line jumps from about

3,000 feet, you'll make your first free fall from about 4,500 feet offering a whopping five seconds of free fall time. As each week goes by you'll jump from increasingly higher altitudes, finally working your way up to about 9,000 or 10,000 feet and about 45-50 seconds of free fall time.

A complete static line training program, which may include about 15-20 jumps before you are off "student status" and certified to jump without supervision, will cost about $1,500.

## Tandem skydiving

Strapped to the front of a trained and experienced instructor with a specially designed two-person canopy and harness, tandem jumping is a reassuring way to make your maiden jump. Your instructor will pull the rip-cord for you, but you will get a chance to steer the canopy and enjoy 40 or more seconds of free fall at 120 mph tightly secured to an expert instructor.

> *Tandem is a reassuring way to make your maiden jump.*

Shortly after a brief ground session, the Siamese twin-like pair — you and the instructor — board the plane and while ascending to altitude, usually 8,000-10,000 feet, you will physically link your jump harnesses, front to back using strong metal carbiners and nylon webbing.

When the two jumpers are linked, they will wiggle to the aircraft's door, and once over the drop zone the joined instructor and student will exit and free fall for nearly a minute, then the jump master will pull the rip-cord and the two will silently fly for about three to four minutes under the

deployed canopy as the instructor demonstrates steering the overhead wing. "Tandem jumping is a great way to try the sport," says Werle.

## Accelerated Free Fall

"Today more and more students graduate from a tandem jumping experience to accelerated free fall where two instructors dive with you, firmly holding on to you when you leave the aircraft at 10,000 or more feet," says Werle. With an instructor on each side, you get hands-on expert assistance and instruction in stabilizing your body, or flying, during your minute of free fall."

"All three of you depart the aircraft at the same time with your instructors firmly hanging on to your harness during the entire free fall, offering instruction and directions for deployment of the canopy. It's great, if you should have a problem, one of the instructors can pull your ripcord and guide you. Even with this technique, all students wear an automatic activation device that can deploy the canopy at a preset minimum altitude."

> *Training begins with about five hours of ground school*

As with static line training, accelerated free fall students begin with about five hours of ground training covering safety and emergency procedures so that in the remote chance something happens to both of your expert instructors, you'll know what to do. AFF is the best vehicle for those who want to solo jump and it's also the safest according to the USPA. "Many believe the ground school helps make the AFF very safe because you are forced to think like a skydiver from the very beginning," says Jerry Werle.

With three or four jumps logged accompanied by two instructors, many students start jumping with only one instructor, which of course lowers costs, but still helps to rapidly build supervised time and skills development.

Usually after 10 or 12 one-instructor jumps, students are approved to solo jump, graduate from student status, and no longer require air-to-air supervision. The AFF approach, which includes all jumps and the cost of two jump masters, will run about $1,500 to $2,000.

## More training

*A good main parachute and steerable reserve can cost nearly $2,000.00*

All three of the jump and training methods above can take you to the next stage of training to obtain your Class A, or basic, license. "Typically beginners need about 20-30 jumps before they reach the Class A license," says Werle, "this license, along with your USPA membership, qualifies you for USPA insurance, and is your ticket to really learn.

You will be packing your own chute and you will be making unsupervised practice jumps, and, most importantly, you'll be free to travel to other drop zones."

Written tests, more jumps, and more training will move you

along to additional licenses and levels of expertise.

## Equipment

As with all risk sports, when you buy — buy the best. Usually after 20 jumps you'll be interested in buying your own

equipment and you will indeed pay for quality, in fact, a main parachute can cost nearly $1,000; a good steerable reserve is about $900; the rig and harness can run about $900; altimeter $175; helmet and jump suit $250; and goggles about $15.

Used equipment is available, often jump schools have equipment for sale or rent, but before you buy or jump with it, the equipment should be thoroughly inspected by an experienced rigger and certified.

The Federal Aviation Administration (FAA), in cooperation with the USPA, regulates skydiving equipment, activities and procedures. The FAA has developed standards, Technical Standards Orders (TSO), for all reserve chutes and harnesses.

All canopies that meet TSO standards have been tested to specifications written and adopted by the Parachute Industry Association under the auspices of the Society of Automotive Engineers (SAE) for the FAA.

The modern ram-air style parachutes are engineered to withstand strong forces on their structural integrity, overall reliability, loading dynamics, and descent rates. While you may pack your own main canopy, an FAA-certified parachute rigger is the only one allowed to pack reserve canopies. The reserve must be repacked every 120 days in accordance with FAA regulations.

As mentioned, you can pack your main canopy and it does not have to be certified under the TSO standards program. Main canopy manufacturers rely on their own testing and safety records to sell parachutes.

The primary manufacturers of student model main canopies are: Strong, Para Flight, Precision Aerodynamics, Glide Path International and Performance Design. American makers set the standard for sport parachutes, from safety design to design advances making the canopies reliable and flyable.

Choose a brand name main canopy, fly as many as possible, and talk to jump masters about their canopy preferences.

Under ideal circumstances a good parachute will last for about 1,000 jumps, far less if exposed to sun and dirt. The average size man, at 160 pounds, will want a 180- to 230-square-foot, 9-cell canopy; skydivers over 180 pounds will want a 240- to 320-square-foot, 9-cell model.

# Organizations

## United States Parachuting Association (USPA)
1440 Duke Street
Alexandria, VA 22314
(703) 836-3495
fax: (703) 836-2843

## Canadian Sport Parachuting Association (CSPA)
RR#3 4195 Dunning Road
Navan, Ontario, Canada
K4B 1J1
(613) 835-3731

# USPA Members

## *Illinois*

## Archway Skydiving Center
City Airport Hwy. 4 North
Sparta, IL
(618) 443-2375

## Greater St. Louis PC
Greenville Municipal Airport
Greenville, IL 62246

(314) 576-JUMP

## Hinckley Parachute Center
Route 30
Hinckley, IL 60520
(708) 377-9219

## Illinois Valley Parachute Club
P.O. Box 284
Minier, IL 61759
Tillman Field
(309) 392-9111

## Mid America SPC
Taylorville Airport
Taylorville, IL 62568
(217) 522-2623 or (217) 824-JUMP

## Rock River Valley Skydivers
P.O. Box 1038
Sterling, IL 61081
(815) 625-6188

## Western Illinois Valley Skydivers
Rt. 96 South
Box 167
Niota, IL 62358
(217) 448-4103

## Indiana

**Carmi Para Center**
Carmi Municipal Airport
Route 1
Carmi, IN
(812) 783-1415

**Illiana Skydivers**
Songers Field
Veedersburg, IN
(317) 793-2816; (217) 442-7784

**New Horizons**
Parachute Club
Eaton, IN
(317) 396-9665

**Parachutes and Associates, Inc.**
Frankfort Municipal Airport
SR 28
Frankfort, IN
(317) 654-6188

**Skydive America, Inc.**
RR #4 Box 105
Rockville, IN
(317) 548-2622

**Skydive Anderson**
Ace Airport

Anderson, IN
(317) 642-7392

**Skydive Mentone**
County Road 42
Goshen, IN
(219) 493-1140

## Michigan

**Great Lakes Skydivers**
38042 28th Ave.
Gobles, MI 49055
(616) 628-4892

**Marshall Airport**
Marshall, MI

**Napoleon Skydiving Center**
Napoleon Airport
P.O. Box 708
Napoleon, MI 49261
(517) 536-5252

**Parahawk Parachuting Club**
Marine City Airport
Marine City, MI 48039
(313) 765-3242

**Skydive Hastings**
2995 W. Airport Rd.

Hasting, MI 49058
(616) 948-2665

**Skydive Michigan**
Maple Grove Airport
7080 Sherwood Road
Fowlerville, MI 48836
(517) 546-9953

**Wild Wind Skydivers**
Alma Airport
Alma, MI
(517) 832-5780

## New York

**Finger Lakes Skydivers**
9798 Congress St.
Trumansburg, NY 14886
(607) 869-5601; 387-5225

**Long Island
Skydivers, Inc.**
Spaderos Airport
Montauk Highway
Moriches, NY 11940
(516) 653-9184

**Malone Parachute Club**
Malone Dufort Airport
Malone, NY
(518) 483-6314; 483-4407

**Rochester Skydivers**
3400 County Line Road,
Rt 272 N
Brockport, NY 14470
(716) 638-8710

**Sky One Skydiving Center**
Curtis Airfield
Teuscher Road
Verona, NY 13478
(315) 363-9275

**Skydive Long Island, Inc.**
91 Montauk Hwy.
East Moriche, NY 11940
(516) 878-JUMP

**The Ranch Parachute
Club Ltd.**
Gardiner Airport
Gardiner, NY
(914) 255-4033; 255-9538

**Wood Air Sports**
Stormville Airport
Stormville, NY
(914) 227-9718; (203) 869-
0787

## Ohio

**Akron Skydivers, Inc.**
Skypark Airport

3071 Greenwich Road
Wadsworth, OH 44281
(216) 762-DIVE; 628-2906

**Alliance Sport
Parachute Club**
237 West Main St.
East Palestine, OH 44413
(216) 426-2565; 426-4372

**Canton Air Sports**
Martin Airport
5367 E. Center Dr NE
Canton, OH 44721
(216) 452-0560

**Cleveland Sport
Parachute Center**
Rt #422
Geauga County
Parkan, OH
(216) 548-4511

**Grand Lake Skydiving**
Lakefield Airport
6177 State Route 219
Celina, OH 45822
(419) 268-2190

**Skydive B.G., Inc.**
P.O. Box 311
Bowling Green., OH 43402
(419) 352-5200

**Skydive Greene
County, Inc.**
177 S. Monroe Siding Road
Xenia, OH 45385
(513) 372-0700

**TopFun Skydiving**
Miller Airport
North Venton, OH
(218) 821-0340

**Waynesville Sky
Sports, Inc.**
Waynesville Airport
4925 N. State Rt. #42
Waynesville, Oh 45068
(800) 678-JUMP

## Pennsylvania

**AFF East/
Skydive Chambersburg**
Municipal Airport
Chambersburg, PA
(800) 526-3497

**Endless Mountain
Skydivers, Inc.**
RD #2 Box 263
Waymart, PA 18472
(717) 937-4317

**Erir Skydiving Center**

5830 Seneca St.
Elma, PA 14059
(716) 674-8543

**Freefall Adventure, Inc.**
Tandem City
New Hanover Airport
Gilbertsville, PA
(215) 644-7760

**Maytown SPC**
Donegal Airpark
Rd. 1
Marietta, PA 17547
(717) 653-9980

**Mifflin County
Skydivers, Inc.**
Mifflin County Airport
Three Cent Lane
Reedsville, PA 17084
(814) 237-1737

**Mon-Yough
Skydivers, Inc.**
J.T. Willie Airport
Worthington, PA 16262
(412) 297-3690

**Morgantown
Parachute Center**
P.O. Box 253
Morgantown, PA 19543

(215) 286-6601

**Northeast Pennsylvania
Ripcords, Inc.**
Cold Springs Farm
Sugarloft, PA 18249
(717) 788-2476

**Presque Isle Skydivers**
Erie International Airport
P.O. Box 8564
Presque Isle, PA 16505
(814) 838-3084

**The Freefall Farm**
Grimes Airport
371 Airport Rd.
Bethel, PA 19507
(215) 343-3318

## Wisconsin

**Baldwin SPC, Inc.**
Baldwin, WI
(715) 684-3416; (612) 227-6486

**Green Bay Skydivers, Inc.**
Pulaski Airport
Pulaski, WI
(414) 822-5010; 434-0337

**Northeast Wisconsin**

**Skydivers**
Rt. #1 Hwy. 54
Shiocton, WI 54170
(414) 986-3212; 498-2298

**Para-Naut, Inc.**
Hwy 21
Oshkosh, WI
(414) 685-5122

**Seven Hills Skydivers, Inc.**
Hwy. 73
Township of York
Center, WI
(414) 623-2838; (608) 244-5252

**Sky Knights**
East Troy Airport
East Troy, WI 53120
(414) 642-9494; 642-9933

**St. Croix Valley
Skydiving Club**
St. Croix Valley Airport
Osceola, WI
(715) 294-4262; (612) 433-3633

**Superior Skydivers**
Bong Municipal Airport
Superior, WI
(715) 392-8811; 394-4612

**Wisconsin Skydivers, Inc.**

Aero Park Airport
W 204 N. 5022 Lannon Rd.
Menomonee falls, WI 53051
(414) 252-3434

# Books and Magazines

The Parachute Manual by Don Poynter, ($49.95), is 592 pages with 2,200 photos and drawings from Para Publishing, P.O. Box 4232 Santa Barbara, CA 93140. (800) PARA PUB.

Skydiving, A Dictionary, by Bill FitzSimmons, Fodderstack Press, P.O. Box 38 Flint Hill, VA 22627.

The Parachute Manual Volume II, by Don Poynter, ($49.95), is 416 pages with 821 photos from Para Publishing (1985).

Parachuting, The Skydiver's Handbook by Don Poynter, ($19.95), is 400 pages with 260 illustrations, Para Publishing.

Skydiving Magazine, (monthly), P.O. Box 1520, DeLand, FL 32721.

Parachuting Manual for Accelerated Freefall, by Jan Meyers, ($3.95), is 36 pages, soft cover.

Parachute Rigger Study Guide, by Deborah Blackmon, ($14.95), 72 pages.

Parachutist Magazine (monthly) from USPA.

CHAPTER 11 **Soaring**

To fly as the hawk and the eagles fly has been man's dream for centuries. Today's sailplanes make soaring flight even higher and faster than the best raptor, using only an invisible force of nature to stay safely aloft.

On your first flight your left hand will be a bit shaky, but stretch it out and grab the golfball-size red tow rope release knob, its shaft between your fingers, and as the tow plane ahead bores a hole in the sky pulling you to 2,000 feet, firmly pull. The sport is called "soaring" and you quickly discover why as the thunking release sound of the tow-plane rope lets the nose of the sailplane rise and you bank sharply to the right. The tow plane banks sharply to the left, clearing away all the bonds of earth.

"First-time pilots can now release the breath they've been unknowingly holding for a thousand feet...and begin to relax...and feel the exhilaration of the sport as the narrow unpowered plane levels and begins to seek out rising columns of air, called thermals," says Chuck Mange, treasurer of the

Northwest Soaring Club in Frankfort, Michigan. "Unlike power pilots, busy at work in their machines monitoring gauges, adjusting dials and mixtures and turning switches and worrying like a bus driver...soaring pilots are far more interested in the trip than the destination."

Instead of passively enjoying the countryside or the sky, you will actively search the air for things such as birds and the maturity of cumulus clouds, and you'll gain respect for areas on the ground that can help or hinder you in meeting the continuing challenge of staying aloft.

Once you've stopped cranking your neck about sucking in the view with each breath, you are likely to fall in love with the intellectual challenge of soaring. "With gravity telling you that a machine weighing 1,000 pounds, with no engine, has no business staying afloat, pilots quickly learn that the sun and the wind and the air have invisible forces far stronger than gravity. And it is up to you to make the most of these forces," says Mange.

He also reminds everyone that the best soaring in the Great Lakes is at Frankfort where you can ride a mix of thermals and cruise along the beautiful northwest coast of Lake Michigan, near Traverse Bay and Mission Point.

## You'll need a lift

If you want to stay in the air you'll need lift, or our old friend gravity will prevail. "The best sailplane drivers seem to have a magical ability to identify lift. They watch the ground for texture and heat, observe the winds and carefully examine the flight of even the tiniest bird, seeking subtle clues as to where the best lift can be found that can be used to keep the tiny plane skyward," says Mange, who is an avid year-round Great Lakes area flyer.

There are three general types of lift: thermal, wave and ridge. Thermal lift is simply warm air rising from the ground that has been heated by the sun. The heat makes the air rise. Often, blacktop parking lots really give off lots of warm rising air which pilots can skillfully use to propel the sailplane. Thermals can be tiny shafts of rising air, narrow turbulent shafts, or large gentle masses of warm rising air.

Ridge lift is created when steady winds blow against a mountain range or large hills. When the wind hits the side of the hills or mountains it bounces upward. Thus, pilots can ride this deflected wind along ridges for many miles.

Wave lift, not commonly found in the Great Lakes region, is when a large air mass spills over the top of a mountain range and hits the valley floor where it then bounces upward, sometimes rising for miles. Waves are the strongest form of lift and can sometimes produce enough lift to permit spectacular ascents of 2,000 feet per minute, reaching altitudes of 30,000 feet or more. Flying the wave is the ultimate experience and is why upstate New York pilots are amount the luckiest in the region.

## Becoming a glider pilot

"If you have about $1,500 bucks and if you are at least 14 years old you can qualify for your first solo flight," says Mange. If you aren't a youngster you can still learn and have fun, actually senior pilots are in the majority, many with thousands of hours of soaring time logged. So any age and just about any income level can participate. Your first ride, which will include plane rental, towing service and professional instruction can cost less than $60. With an additional $1,200 to $1,500 you can complete a private license. You can go at your own speed with many people taking only two or three lessons a month, and it is quite possible to go from start to solo in a typical two-week vacation — if the weather is agreeable.

"Many soaring clubs have planes and instructors, and low overhead due to volunteers. Often beginners can find terrific bargains by joining and using a soaring club's resources," says Mange, a long-time club officer.

## Training and your license

As you climb into the typical two-place glider you'll be cramped and will start wondering when toy companies began building gliders. They are narrow and seem ungainly. As soon as the glider lifts off the runway, pulled by a throaty tow plane, your perceptions will change. The glider is most at home in the air, above the birds. It is a sleek, polished Fiberglas creature at home in its element.

After your demo ride and during the early phase of training, qualifying to solo, you will fly under the guidance of a certified flight instructor in a two-place, dual-control glider. It will typically take 25-35 flights before you are ready to solo. Many flying clubs are dedicated to instruction, offering cost savings and a number of qualified instructors willing to give lessons in the evening or on weekends.

As with traditional flight schools, clubs operate low performance, highly forgiving gliders, such as the Schweizer 232s or 233s. They have a solid glide ratio of 24:1, a long way from the 40:1 or greater glide ratio of slippery Fiberglass performance sailplanes. Although more difficult to fly, the high performance planes become everyone's dream ship and many seasoned glider pilots advise serious novice aviators to train in the best and fastest gliders. In large part, it is an economy of scale decision, dependent upon what's available in your area.

## The rating and license

After seven hours or so of solo flight, most beginning pilots have really sharpened their coordination and judgment, gaining knowledge of weather, safety planning and skills needed for more challenging flights. This minimum of seven solo hours is also a requirement of the FAA to get your private pilot glider license, followed by a written exam and an in-flight test.

The private pilot glider license, as with all beginning ratings, is really your ticket to learn. Soon you'll be chasing thermals, ridge soaring, flying to greater and greater altitudes, using the VHF radio and landing at other airports or in fields where you then take your glider apart for safe storage in a trailer during the drive home.

## The equipment

A sailplane has been described as a piece of living sculpture that a pilot wears to climb invisible mountains in the sky. Beyond the mystical, magical beauty of the plane, seemingly shaped by the wind itself, today's sailplane is a wonder of aerodynamic efficiency. More advances have been made in sailplanes in the past 20 years than in any other area of flight.

> **A sailplane has been described as a "piece of living sculpture that a pilot wears to climb invisible mountains in the sky."**

Since the 1960s, modern sailplanes have pioneered the use of composites, such as Fiberglas-epoxy and carbon fiber-epoxy. These light, strong, and highly moldable materials have enabled designers of the latest sailplanes to create very smooth, low-drag and lightweight wings, tails and fuselages. They are finished to within micro inches, and use higher performance, thinner airfoils developed to take advantage of these materials, all in the interest of reduced drag and increased aerodynamic efficiency.

Contrary to popular belief, sailplanes are not flimsy vehicles that float on the wind. Modern sailplanes are actually built to withstand stresses (G-forces) comparable to a commercial airliner. Performing sailplane aerobatics that put maximum stresses on an aircraft, is among the fastest growing segments of the sport of soaring, according to the Soaring Society of America, Inc.

Expensive racing sailplanes also carry up to 400 pounds of water in special bags in the wings. Used for ballast to improve penetration speeds, the water can be dumped should soaring conditions grow weak, thus allowing greater climb perfor-

mance. The water is always dumped before landing, so keep a look out for low flying sailplanes.

A key measurement of efficiency is achieved glide ratio, a high performance glider with a ratio of 60:1 can fly 60 miles (in still air) from a height of one mile. Sailplanes are airplanes in every respect, with all controls and instruments, except they rarely have motors, although small efficient engines and improved performance are allowing some designers to include a small retractable motor located behind the pilot.

Racing sailplanes are equipped with basic aircraft instrumentation such as altimeter, compass, airspeed indicator and radios. Additionally, sophisticated computers measure glider performance and predict speed-to-fly for optimum performance. Special, sensitive instruments called variometers detect and measure vertical air currents to indicate rising air in which sailplanes climb. Many racing sailplanes can fly as slow as 45 mph when flying between thermals to over 140 mph in high-speed cruise. Many racers average more than 80 mph.

Many soaring clubs, like the Frankfort, Michigan club offer 2,000-foot-high tows for $11 to $13. Many of the clubs have a small monthly membership fee, which covers the cost of tow plane maintenance and so on.

# Soaring Services

## *Canada*

**Royal Canadian
Flying Clubs**
1815 Alta Vista Drive
#103 Ottawa, Ontario  K1G
3Y6

## *Illinois*

**Chicago Glider Club**
26045 W. Airport Road
Minooka, IL 60447
(815) 467-9861

**Hinckley Soaring**
Box 868
Hinckley, IL 60520
(815) 286-7200

**Illini Glider Club**
101 Transportation Blvd.
Urbana, IL 61801
(217) 333-7651

**Park Forest
South Aviation**
Box 104
Richton Park, IL 60471
(708) 748-3341

**Sky Soaring, Inc.**
1502 Chapel CT.
Northbrook, IL 60062
(708) 272-0105 or 683-2820

**St. Louis Soaring
Association**
36 Innsbuck Lane
Shilholm, IL 62221
(618) 624-2542

**Wabash Valley Soaring**
Box 287
Lawrenceville, IL 62439
(618)  943-2076  or  (812)
882-2829

**Windy City Soaring**
10302 S. Napier-Romeo Rd.
Plainfield, IL 60544
(708) 759-2046

## *Indiana*

**Central Indiana Soaring**
Society, Inc.
8105 Valley Farm Trail
Indianapolis, IN 46214
(317) 291-7348

**Michiana Soaring Society**
515 W. Lowell
Mishawaka, IN 46545

(219) 259-2169

## New York

**Aero Soaring Club, Inc.**
Box 107
Mayville, NY 14757
(716) 753-5125 or 664-6892

**Glider Pilot
Ground School**
69 Rhea Rd.
Crescent, Rochester, NY 14615
(716) 865-9511

**Harris Hill Soaring Corp.**
607 Post Creek Rd.
Beaver Dams, NY 14812
(607) 739-7899

**Iroquois Soaring
Association**
6433 Karlen Rd.
Rome, NY 13440
(315) 339-0009

**Long Island Soaring
Association**
1247 Ledham Ct.
Merrick, NY 11566
(516) 223-9456

**Mohawk Soaring Club**
57 Wakefield Court
Delmar, NY 12054
(413) 458-8650

**National Soaring Museum**
Harris Hill Rd. #3
Elmira NY 14903
(607) 734-3128

**Niagara Soaring Club**
3767 Moyer Rd.
North Tonawanda, NY 14120
(716) 693-1823

**Rochester Soaring Club**
125 Parkmeadow Dr.
Pittsford, NY 14534
(716) 334-7985 or 235-0625

**Saratoga Soaring
Association**
17 Vichy Drive
Saratoga Springs, NY 12866
(518) 587-1957

**Schweizer Soaring School**
P.O. Box 147
Elmira, NY 14902
(607) 739-3821

**Sky Sailors, Inc.**

Suffolk Co. Airport
Rust Avenue Bldg. 313
Westhampton Beach, NY
11978
(516) 288-5858

**Thermal Ridge
Soaring, Inc.**
115 Kittell Rd.
Fayetteville, NY 13066
(315) 446-4545

**Triple Cities
Soaring Society**
Box 7063
Endicott, NY 13760
(607) 757-9181

**Valley Soaring**
42 Lenape Trail
Wayne, NJ 07470
(201) 696-8823

**Wurtsboro Flight
Service, Inc.**
50 Barone Rd.
Wurtsboro, NY 12790
(914) 888-2791

## Ohio

**Caesar Creek Soaring Club**
5385 Elbon Rd.

Waynesville, OH 45068
(513) 932-7627

**Central Ohio Soaring
Association**
Box 29349
Columbus, OH 43229
(614) 888-4128

**Cleveland Soaring
Society, Inc.**
20550 University Blvd. #211
Shaker Heights, OH 44122
(216) 285-9378

**Fun County Soaring**
525 S. Main
Wellington, OH 44090
(216) 647-2050

**Lane's Lebanon**
Air Service
2460 Greentree Rt.
Lebanon, OH 45036
(513) 932-7966

**Northern Ohio
Soaring Association**
400 W. High St. E.
Palestine, OH 44413
(216) 426-1923

**Soaring Thunderbirds**

710 Mentor Rd.
Akron, OH 44303
(216) 864-9114

## Michigan

**Adrian Soaring Club, Inc.**
34218 Case Court
Farmington, MI 48335
(313) 447-5057

**Benz Aviation, Inc.**
3148 S. State Road
Ionia, MI 48846
(616) 527-9070

**Kittyhawk Soaring Club**
2444 Lake in the Woods Blvd.
#926
Ypsilanti, MI 48198

**Marshall Soaring Club**
15096 A Drive North
Marshall, MI 49068
(616) 781-3996 or (517) 783-1510

**Northwest Soaring Club**
of Frankfort
Box 88
Frankfort, MI 49635
(616) 352-9160

**Sandhill Soaring Club**
Box 2021
Ann Arbor, MI 48106
(313) 761-1132 or 498-2075

**The Vultures, Inc.**
1878 Tahquamenon Ct.
Bloomfield Hills, MI 48302
(313) 851-0185

## Minnesota

**Glider Club, Inc.**
Municipal Airport
Albert Lea, MN 56007
(507) 373-0608

**Minnesota Soaring Club**
Carleton Airport
Stanton, MN 55018
(507) 645-4030

**Red Wing Soaring Association**
Box 10828
White Bear, MN 55110
(612) 724-8280

## Pennsylvania

**Butler Soaring Club**
951 Wellesley Rd.
Pittsburgh, PA 15206

(415) 441-4589

**Cloudniners**
2501 Trinity Ct.
Chester Springs, PA 19425
(215) 524-0160

**Country Aviation, Inc.**
Box 218
Erwinna, PA 18920
(215) 847-8401

**Keystone Gliderport**
RR1, Box 414
Julian, PA 16844
(814) 355-2483

## *Wisconsin*

**West Bend Air, Inc.**
Box 409
West Bend, WI 53095
(414) 334-5603

**EAA Air Museum**
11311 W. Forest Home Ave.
Franklin, WI 52132

# Organizations

**Soaring Society of America (SSA)**
P.O. Box E
Hobbs, NM 88241-1308  (505) 392-1177

*More and more senior pilots are taking up the challenge of soaring.*

## Soaring facts

• There are 20,000 FAA licensed glider pilots in the United States.

• More than 100,000 glider pilots fly worldwide.

• There are more than 180 soaring clubs in America.

• There are more than 150 commercial gliderports and soaring supply businesses in the United States.

• More than $19 million is spent on soaring in the United States annually.

• An average glider pilot spends $1,000 a year on soaring and may spend in excess of $20,000 on a sailplane purchase.

• A new plane costs between $20,000 and $40,000.

• There are 4,000 registered sailplanes in the United States.

• About 1,000 of them are trainers and 1,000 are high

performance models.
• Soaring exists in every state.

## National Records

*Straight Distance:* Michael Koerner of California, 902.95 miles.

*Out & Return Distance:* Tom Knauff of Pennsylvania, 1,023.42 miles.

*Altitude:* Robert Harris, 49,009 feet.

*Speed over 100 KM Triangle:* Tom Knauff of Pennsylvania, 116.1 mph.

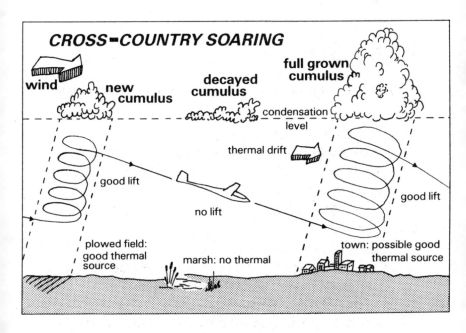

# Books and Magazines

Soaring Magazine
SSA monthly magazine
P.O. Box E
Hobbs, NM 88241
(505) 392-1177, fax (505) 392-8154

Practical Wave Flying ($12.95)
Lenticular Publishing
Box 3842
Englewood, CO 80155-3842

Soaring Pilot Magazine ($20/yr.)
R.R. 1 Box 414
Julian, PA 16844
(814) 355-2483

Handbook of Soaring Meteorology, Chas. Lindsay ($19.95)
4404 44th Ave.
South Minneapolis, MN 55406
(612) 722-1180

Sailplane and Gliding Magazine (British, $35/yr. US)
British Gliding Association
Kimberley House, Vaugh Way
Leicester, LE1 4SE, England

Free Flight Magazine ($22/yr. US)
Suite 306
1355 Bank St.
Ottawa, Ontario, Canada K1H 8K7

Technical Soaring Magazine ($24/yr. member)
SSA P.O. Box E
Hobbs, NM 88241
(505) 392-1177

# CHAPTER 12

# Ultralights

The magic of simple flight — wind in the face, bugs on the teeth, an unobstructed view, and exploring the countryside at 40 mph — is a powerful and compelling experience. Ease of operation, storage, low cost, and increasing safety are just a few more reasons ultralight flying in the Great Lakes area is the fastest growing, powered flying sport.

"Competition, an improved regulatory environment, a network of more than a dozen clubs in the region, skilled instructors, and the proliferation of new ultralight vehicle designs is increasing membership in the U.S. Ultralight Association," says Jim Stephenson, of Marshall, Michigan, the association's region six chairman.

An engineer, Stephenson says aircraft builders, skilled traditional pilots and thrill seekers are drawn to the sport for slightly different reasons, but the mix of talents and personalities is dynamic and the sport's greatest strength. The USUA has nearly 7,000 members.

## Learning to fly ultralights

"Fifteen years ago or so many ultralights were rickety crafts, often the result of a shade-tree mechanic approach to building and design," says Stephenson. "Today, dozens of very safe, high-tech designs are offered in kit form, many of which take 100 or less hours to assemble. You can also buy completely assembled aircraft that have been tested and tried."

> *A with most thrill sports, modern equipment is safe, it's the people using the equipment we worry about.*

As with most thrill sports, modern equipment is safe, it's the people using the equipment we worry about. A thorough understanding of the sport, aircraft and safety rules is the best insurance for safety. And that begins with a top instructor.

Because the fragile ability to fly is not something humans are born with, the lessons and habits we learn from our instructors can mean the difference between a lifetime of safe flight or deadly danger. "It is the ultralight flight instructor, with their experience, knowledge and skills who educate us to the subtleties of control input and knowledge of airspace we are flying in," says Stephenson. "Their almost inhuman patience and understanding, both on the ground and in the air, provides the type of training and lessons needed to save us from our uncertain mistakes as we learn this new skill."

"In the early 1980's the FAA enacted regulations (FAR Part 103) to govern ultralights and their operation," says Stephenson. "The FAA established minimum standards and mandated the industry to 'self-regulate' the flying community and maintain a comprehensive registry of pilots and aircraft." Using FAA circulars and special rules developed for ultralight operations, industry-wide safety standards were established and implemented for pilot training, vehicle registration and marking. There are about 18,000 records in the registry.

The instructors listed later are registered through USUA and have passed written tests and practical flight tests to confirm their knowledge and skill of the fundamentals of teaching emergency and normal maneuvers, pilot examining, and program administration specific to ultralights. All USUA-registered instructors carry a FAA training exemption and registration card. When looking for an instructor, ask to seek their credentials. The value of your training depends on it.

Weekend ground school instructors should also be skilled, USUA registered flight trainers. There are nearly 300 current instructors who can help fulfill your dream to fly an ultralight.

No written tests, no medical certificates, and the vehicles are not required to be registered. Because of this "loose" training and certification criteria in the FAA regulation, budding ultralight pilots should find the best training, learn as much as possible — in fact some recommend taking a traditional private pilots course — and get considerable dual instruction combined with respect and vigilance in operation.

## USUA ultralight airmen registration

Because the FAA has mandated that the industry self-regulate, the USUA has established training criteria and a registration system that is reasonable and recommended, but technically not required.

USUA membership is required to participate in this program.

*Student:* You must be 14 years old. The requirement for solo flight includes competency on the "Ultralight Pre-solo Written Test," five hours of flight training from a USUA instructor, and an endorsement from your instructor. The applicant also must successfully demonstrate to a USUA instructor the ability to perform the tasks of solo flying, including: 1) preflight check; 2) ground handling; 3) takeoffs and landings; 4) traffic patterns; 5) flight at minimum controllable airspeed; and 6) emergency procedures.

The solo flight destination must also be approved. The solo endorsement is valid for 90 days or until the student registers as a pilot.

USUA student pilots are required to maintain a logbook that records aeronautical training and experience.

To qualify as a USUA ultralight pilot you must fulfill the above requirements, solo under supervision, be 16 years old, pass the "Ultralight Pilot Written Test" administered by a USUL instructor, have 10 hours of flight and/or ground school, including three hours of supervised takeoffs and landings, and have completed at least 25 takeoffs and landings.

A skill test is also required after successful completion of your written test, which requires successful completion of an oral and flight examination.

# Buying an ultralight

Because ultralight flying is a more affordable alternative to general aviation — and certainly more thrilling — many future flyers will be able to afford an ultralight vehicle early in the experience. Most ultralights will actually cost less than a new car.

Dave Loveman, owner and operator of Buzzman Enterprises, writes in Ultralight Flying Magazine that there are many factors involved in evaluating and purchasing safe and reliable ultralight aircraft. Loveman recommends you buy your machine from a manufacturer that has been in business for at least five years, has an aircraft that has been in production for at least three years and has sold more than 100 kits (units). Buy a three-axis control system or a weight-shift control system in trike models (tricycle landing gear).

Loveman also recommends the popular Rotax engine, which ranges in size from 28 to 80 horsepower. Zenoah, Hirth, Preceptor, Mosler, Arrow, AMW and Kawasaki are also excellent engines, but he believes each have minor limitations when judged next to the Rotax. Buy from a manufacturer that produces a two-place trainer.

Buy an ultralight that can cruise cross-country at 50-55 mph. Is there a dealership within 100 miles? Check the model's overall safety record and talk to as many owners as possible of the model you are considering.

Some companies claim that their kits can be assembled in as little as 60 hours, and that may be true of an experienced builder. Often, according to experts, it will take more time to assemble your purchase than is advertised.

A single seater can cost (without engine) from as little as $4,000 to $15,000, or more. Two-seaters can cost (without engine) from $8,000 to $20,000. Trikes (they have tricycle landing gear, without engine) cost between $8,000 and $14,000. Powered chutes, a ram-air style paraglider-like parachute with a single to two-seat vehicle and a motor slung underneath can cost under $10,000.

# Ultralight Flight In-structors-USUA

## *Illinois*

**Mike Harrison**
Mt. Auburn, IL
(217) 692-2567

**Jamie Kee**
E. Peoria, IL
(309) 694-2339

**Richard Davies**
West Chicago, IL
(708) 293-7610

**Gregory Peters**
Arlington Heights, IL
(708) 818-0343

**Jeff Tideman**
Villa Park. IL
(708) 834-9165

**William Nichols**
S. Benoit, IL
(815) 389-3559

**Ervin Kincannon**
Dakota, IL

(815) 563-4551

**William L. Ipema**
New Lenox, IL
(815) 485-0757

## *Indiana*

**David K. Belswanger**
Wolcottville, IN
(219) 351-2516

**Everett D. Currie**
Decatur, IL
(219) 724-9582

**Daniel Grimm**
Newburgh, IN
(812) 853-5252

**Phil Larsh**
Colfax, IN
(317) 324-2424

**Harold Kiser**
Kokomo, IN
(317) 457-1311

**Scott S. Mullarkey**
Carmel, IN
(317) 844-1423

**Charles Smith**

Mt. Vernon, IN
(812) 838-6351

**David Rogers**
Sheridan, IN
(317) 628-2691

## Michigan

**Leslie Dobson**
Kalamazoo, MI
(616) 349-4985

**Mark Kriewall**
Romeo, MI
(313) 247-8666

**Barry Sutton**
Metamore, MI
(313) 667-3675

**Brian Champagne**
Richmond, MI
(313) 784-5535

**Jon Jacobs**
Samaria, MI
(313) 856-7103

**Charles Story**
Haslett, MI
(517)655-5858

**Patrick Schultheis**
Kalamazoo, MI
(616) 375-2203

**John Chapman**
Kalamazoo, MI
(616) 383-2016

## Minnesota

**Jerry Scrabeck**
Rochester, MN
(507) 289-3495

**Dan A. Mattsen**
Corcoran, MN
(612) 420-3405

**Dale Funk**
Wanamingo, MN
(507) 642-8360

**Larry Lee Bowman**
S. St. Paul, MN
(612) 777-0781

## New York

**Robert Cannioto**
Horsehead, NY
(607) 962-8361

**George Roscoe**

New City, NY
(914) 634-0167

**Vincent Rizzi, Jr.**
Highland, NY
(914) 691-7882

**Joseph Acoveno**
Westbrookville, NY
(914) 754-8069

**Richard Platler**
Holland Platet, NY
(315) 865-8298

**Gunnar Graubaum**

Millertown, NY
(518) 789-6550

**William Lock**
Horsehead, NY
(607) 739-0178

## Ohio

**Barney Schwenzer**
Mayfield Village, OH
(216) 449-3938

**Robertt Essell**
Ravenna, OH
(216) 297-5495

**John Williams**
Geneva, OH
(216) 428-2788

**Leslie K. Alderman**
St Clairsville, OH
(614) 695-5686

## Pennsylvania

**William Hall**
Murrysville, PA
(412) 327-2288

**Donald Blank**
West Middlesex, PA
(412) 662-2020

**Curtis Hughes**
North Huntington, PA
(412) 672-2165

**William Johnson**
Canonsburg, PA
(412) 745-4040

## Wisconsin

**Ricky L. Hill**
Bristol, WI
(414) 857-7356

**John M. Ward**

Bristol, WI
(414) 857-7560

**Thomas Kretschman**
Verona, WI
(608) 845-6230

**Ronald Jinsky**
Beloit, WI
(608) 362-1731

**Kenley Snyder**
Wisconsin Rapids, WI
(715) 423-1128

**George Karamittis**
Berline, WI
(414) 361-1618

**Ken Smith**
Bailey's Harbor, WI
(414) 839-2087

**Graydon Gray**
Montello, WI
(608) 296-2238

**Deborah Shuman**
Camp Douglas, WI
(608) 427-3561

**Ron Brooks**
Waupaca, WI

(715) 258-3403

**Daniel Marlenga**
Schofield, WI
(715) 359-5990

# USUA Clubs and AOOA Flightparks

## *Illinois*

**Sport Planes, Inc.**
Wm Ipema
1338 Schoolhouse Rd.
New Lenox, IL 60451
(815) 485-0757

**Dewey Long**
RR 2 Box 128
Pana, IL 62557
(217) 226-4203

**Fox Valley Flying Club**
Jim McGovern
P.O. Box 23
Montgomery, IL 60538
(815) 264-7919

**North Dock
Field Flightpark**
Tommy Georges
1730 Melrose

Springfield, IL 62703
(217) 525-4986

**Heart of Illinois
Ultralight Club**
Janet Fancher
413 W. Elm
Mason City, IL 62664
(217) 482-3401

## *Indiana*

**Grass Roots Ultralight
Flyers, Inc.**
Barbara Rodgers
8313 E. 400 S Road
Greentown, IN 46936
(317) 628-2691

**Hoosier Flyers**
Carls Larsh
RR 1 Box 149
Colfax, IN 46035
(317) 324-2424

**Indiana's First**
Bob Sunderland
6122 U.S. 33 West
Fort Wayne, IN 46818
(219) 489-6300

**Larsh Flightpark**
Phil Larsh

R. 1 Box 149
Colfax, IN 46035
(317) 324-2424

## Michigan

**Marshall Cloud Busters**
Bert Rosenau
16505 B Drive South
Marshall, MI 49680
(616) 781-4951

**Michigan**
**Ultralight Association**
Don Niles
5400 Duffield Rd.
Swartz Creek, MI 48473
(313) 621-4202

**Michiana Barfing Dogs**
Bill Woverton
2835 Geyer Rd.
Niles, MI 49120
(616) 695-6657

**Alamo Air Force**
Curly Hackenberg
15420 M-216
Three Rivers, MI 49093
(616) 279-2026

**Michigan Ultralight Eagles**
Malcolm Brubaker

Mellon Field
4229 W. McNally Rd.
Coleman, MI 48618
(517) 631-9503

## Minnesota

**Minnesota Ultralight**
**Association**
Gregg Ellsworth
2195 Bonnie Lane
Golden Valley, MN 55422
(612) 588-8014

## New York

**Ultralight Airforce**
Mickey Rowe
240 Rafferty Rd.
Painted Post, NY 14870
(607) 937-5677

**Southerntier UL**
**of New York**
Thomas Wood
RD. #1, Box 111 Old
Hill Road
Unadilla, NY 13849
(607) 563-2516

**Ramapo Valley**
Ultralight Club
Paul Holtz

22 Ross Avenue
Chestnut Ridge, NY 10977
(914) 623-1445

**UFO of New York-UL Flying**
Dr. Anthony J. Romanazzi
73 Bay Street
Glens Falls, NY 12801
(518) 792-4226

**White Pine Ultralight Flying Club**
Jack Van Camp
14 Elysium Dr.
Ely, NY 89301
(702) 289-4687

## Ohio

**Liberty Airpark**
Bob Essell
6188 State Route 303
Ravena, OH 44266
(216) 297-5495

**North Coast Lite Flyers**
Wayne Keller
6188 State Road
Ravenna, OH 44266
(211) 297-5495

## Pennsylvania

**Western PA Lite
Flyers Society**
Gary R. Silvis
R.D. 6, Box 625
Mt. Plesant, PA 15666
(412) 925-6875

**Lizzard Creek Valley
Aeronauts**
Greg Solt
Box 55
Ashfield, PA 18212
(215) 837-9421

**Pittsburg Ultralight
Club 32**
Charles I. Lynch

Box 1400
Elrama, PA 15038
(412) 384-6372

**Mason Dixon Sport Flyer**
Paul Furst
1227 West Poplar
York, PA 17404
(717) 854-4743

## *Wisconsin*

**Winfield Aviation**
Rick Hill
18300 Winfield Rd.
Bristol, WI 53104
(414) 857-7356

# Organizations

**United States Ultralight**
**Association**
P.O. Box 667
Frederick, MD 21705
(301) 695-9100 or Fax: (301) 695-0763

**Great Lakes Region 6**
Jim Stephenson
P. O. Box 589
Marshall, MI 49068
(616) 781-4021

## Publications

Ultralight/Amateur Aircraft Safety Data Exchange Computer Bulletin Board. The FAA offers a computer bulletin board listing service difficulties for ultralights and home built version. You can report and read service bulletins. Contact Ben Morrow, FAA, ACE-103, 601 E. 12th Street, Kansas City, MO 64106, (816) 426-3580.

Ultralight Airmanship, by Michael Markowski, ($11), USUA, P.O. Box 557, Mt. Aity, MD 21771, (301) 898-5000.

Ultralight Flight, by Michael Markowski, ($14), USUA.

Understanding the Sky: A Sport Pilot's Guide to Flying Conditions, by Dennis Pagen, ($20), USUA.

Powered Ultralight Flying, by Denis Pagen, ($11), USUA.

Powered Ultralight Flying Training Course, by Dennis Pagen, ($10), USUA.

USUA Guidelines for the Operation of Ultralight Vehicles, ($1), USUA.

*Joe Boersma, Great Lakes Regional Director, sails year around.*

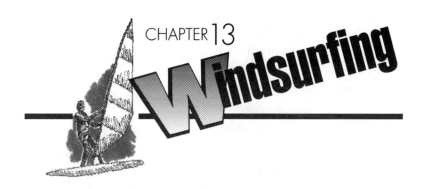

CHAPTER 13

Windsurfing

"**If** you can sail in the Great Lakes, you can sail anywhere...you can use smaller and faster sail boards to cut through the chop or dare to windsurf the edges of a gale," says Joe Boersma, Great Lakes Regional Director of the United States Windsurfing Association. "From Maui to 'the gorge,' Aruba to San Francisco Bay, the Great Lake's huge chop, with back-to-back-to back waves is as challenging as anywhere in North America."

"With the advances in equipment, races, open water crossing, and promotion, the entire Great Lakes region is rapidly becoming a mecca for windsurfers, well sponsored events, outfitters, and quality instruction," says Boersma.

Unlike the placid regular sailing community (sail boats) Great Lakes area windsurfers thrive on technology, constantly improving performance by tinkering with sail configuration, composite or epoxy materials, and fancy mast riggings, says Boersma. "Equipment is getting really fast—the speed record is 51 mph—but at the same time equipment is easier to sail. Beginners now benefit from smaller stable boards and sails, lighter material technology borrowed from aviation, and enthusiastic instruction."

## History

From the first humble "freesail" board built by Newman Derby in 1965 and detailed in Popular Science Magazine, inventors and board sailors spent the next decade modifying the mast, universal connection of the mast to board, alloy riggings, and experimenting with booms, footstraps, sails and fins.

It wasn't until the early 1970s that sailboards began to look like today's sleek craft. Dave Drake, an American sailor, was the first to develop a flexible universal joint to connect the mast to the board so that it could be quickly and safely pivoted to capture the best winds. This innovation even launched the patent of the system that popularize the name "windsurfer."

*All ages love to windsurf.*

Over the years the riggings and sails have changed and improved, but the basic flat board design has survived more to less intact due to its immense stability. In 1973, Hoyle Schweitzer purchased the patent from early equipment, refined the design, and began limited production, which almost immediately couldn't keep up with the demand that was fueled by the California market.

Five years later the widespread adoption of footstraps revolutionize the sport, manufactures flooded the market, and the fact-paced activity spread to five oceans and five continents. Today "radical" boards, with sweeping carved gibes and ultra light materials allow experienced windsurfers to do slalom, jumps, bumps and speed—lots of speed.

# Equipment

"Colorful windsurfers line many Great Lakes' beaches, some rivers, and inland lakes on breezy summer days," says Boersma, "The variety of boards on display is amazing, some narrow and short speedboards, slightly longer slalomboards, and longer flatboards for beginners." The construction and materials used have a direct bearing on prices.

"Plastic boards—polyethylene—are cast from moldings and filled with foam, while more expensive and stronger boards are made from various types of high-grade fiberglass. At the top end, often costing thousands of dollars, are custom air-core, epoxy or honeycomb carbon fiber boards." says Boersma. Custom boards are fit to your height, weight, strength, sail size, and use.

The type of water, wind conditions, and skills are determining factors for the type of board you will ultimately want.

Beginner boards are long and wide, flat-hulled (for stability) and high in volume (thick). These features make learning fun and easier, according to Boersma. Fortunately most boards made today are funboards, and available in student models, usually 350-370 cm in length.

## Sails

Like ordinary sail powered boats, the windsurfer gains forward motion by wind that flows toward the sail and separates about the mast and travels along each side of the sail's surface. Because the sail is curved much like an airplane wing, the wind affects each side differently; on the leeward side the air is accelerated, resulting in a pressure reduction. Conversely, on the windward side the air slows down causing a high pressure zone. This action of high pressure pushing toward the low pressure areas creates the drive that propels the board forward.

The daggerboard (fin) resist sideward movements and ensures that there is forward motion with little lateral drift.

The typical beginners sail will have five to six square meters of surface, which is considered a medium-sized sail, used in light air.

"The windsurfing sail is constructed of a series of shaped panels often made of Dacron or Mylar that is carefully tapered and bonded together," says Boersma. There are soft sails, which have an unsupported luff area, and hard sails with full-length battens that support the entire surface. Soft sails are easier to manage for beginners; hard sails are virtually the standard for all serious recreation or racing windsurfers.

## Harnesses

Windsurfing harnesses come in three styles: chest, seat, and waist, and none of them are designed to provide much buoyancy, and should not be thought of as a personal flotation device.

The harness is really a sailing aid which eases the strain on your arms and back from the stress of hanging onto the sail. A good harness is a great energy saving device that making windsurfing safer and more enjoyable. The large hook at the front of the harness simply clips over a line attached to the boom at about waist level. After you are hooked the harness transfer the pull of the rig through your entire body, instead of your arms. You wouldn't sail long without a quality harness.

The seat harness, when combined with a wet suit and light weight personal floatation device is standard equipment for windsurfers in the Great Lakes region.

## Terminology

**Apparent wind:** the true wind and the wind force created upon the sail surface by the forward movement of the board.

**Battens:** long, thin, fiberglass strip that are bone-like supports structure that keep the sail stiff.

**Bear away:** steering the board away from the wind.

**Beam reach:** sometimes called close reach, is a course 90 degrees to the wind. It is the easiest and fastest type sailing for beginners.

**Broad reach:** this is the fastest point of sailing, typically 120 degrees off the wind. Racers use this angle.

**Camber inducer:** a tuning-fork like mechanism the fits to the leading edge of the sail and acts to stabilize the front edge and luff area in an effort to increase efficiency.

**Cavitation:** often called a spin-out when the fins looses their grip in the water and the back of the board spins out away from its track. Experience sailors can sense the action and slow and steer out of the situation.

**Clew:** the area of the sail at the read end of the boom.

**Close haul:** steering as closely as possible into the wind, usually following about a 45 degree course toward the wind using a series of tacks.

**Edge:** the leading edge of the sail, along with the stiff battens and inducer stabilizer makes the sail more aerodynamically efficient.

**"Eye of the wind:"** direction of the true wind.

**Harness:** there are three types: seat, waist and chest. They distribute the pull of the sail away from the sailor's arms. They allow longer and safer sailing.

**Head to wind:** pointing the nose of the board directly into the wind. The boat will stop and sail will flap freely.

**Hull:** the board when the mast and other rigging removed.

**Leech:** the trailing edge of the sail.

**Planing:** or trimmed, when the board skimmers across the water with the least resistance.

**Rig:** the mast, sail, boom.

**Roach:** an imaginary line that connects the clue to the leech.

**Run:** the farthest point of sailing off the wind, the nose of the board pointing a full 180 degrees downwind.

**Sinker:** a board that can support the weight of the rig and sailor when not in motion.

**Tack:** zig-zagging to make ground upwind.

**Universal joint:** the connection of the mast to the board that allows the mast to be tilted about a plane 360 degrees.

**Wipe out:** pilot error.

## The basics

"My dad is nearly 80 years old and my son is in early elementary school...and I've seen just about every shape and size of people windsurfing," says Boersma, "I think anybody with reasonable balance and coordination can safely practice the sport."

Although you can hop aboard a windsurfer and flounder about learning the techniques, the USWA recommends some brief instruction that includes safety information, and short-cuts to learning how to sail.

## Rigging up

Many sailors say the hardest part of windsurfing is getting the board from the car to the water. Once in the water the windsurfer is easier to handle. Setting up the rig is a simple process and should take about 15 minutes. My instructor took time to demonstrate slipping the mast up the luff sleeve, inserting the mast foot, adjusting the sail, attaching the boom, and inspection of components for excessive wear and proper connection.

Next, neophyte sailors will learn the starting position in shallow water, practicing uphauling the rig, lifting the sail out of the water, balance on the board, and sailing away.

Once you are up on the board, keeping the mast at the original plane, you can adjust your foot position, the sail will quickly power up and you are off. Good schools will have instructors that stay with you at this point and that let you become comfortable in light air, while beginning to introduce steering and tacking techniques. From gibing to beach starts, after a couple days of sailing, you will become very proficient at the basics.

## A few places to go

### *Illinois*

### Chicagoland
Waukegon, with its abundant free parking and chop hopping; Michigan City is laid back, and Warren Dunes in southwestern Michigan are all great places for the Chicago-based sailors to explore. Don't forget Rainbow Beach and the "perfect for practicing" waters near Montrose.

### Evanston
Dempter Beach, near Dawes Park on Lake Michigan is one of the few municipally managed boardsailing locations in the Midwest. No tides, no freighters, no salt water, and a prevailing west/southwest—but it can blow from all directions—is a terrific sailing area where weather tracks often whip up strong winds.

## Michigan

### Grand Haven
Three and-a-half-hours from Detroit or Chicago. "The place to go when the wind blows," has made it a key venue for national competitions. Grand Haven City Park, State Park, or two miles north of town are all great locations with waves that roll in very cleanly.

### Harbor Springs
The most consistent wind in the Great Lakes. Winds fill at about 1 p.m. and peak at sunset, with prevailing winds out of the west and southwest. Visits the friendly sailors at Zoll Street launch or at nearby Petoskey State Park off Highway 31.

### Lake Charlevoix
Quaint and charming, even Ernest Hemingway spent many

summers there enjoying the ideal summer climate, blue waters, small harbors, and connecting channels to Lake Michigan. Mild winds and gentle waters makes this area a very attractive destination for recreational sailors.

### Saginaw Bay

Lake Huron, with plenty of quiet launch sites around the entire rim of the huge bay. Steady winds and the waters can string to life in a short times as weather patterns cross from west to east. Try the Tawas area, north of Bay City.

### South Haven

Convenient parking along three-mile-long beach. Strong winds spring and fall.

### Traverse City

A favorite launch site is Acme Roadside Park, on the east arm, six miles north of Traverse City via North 131. Sailing is good here with all wind except east which is blocked by shoreside bluffs. Ten miles farther north is Elk Rapids, where two public beaches. About 25 minutes from TC is Bingham on Lake Leelanau. Traverse City State Park has a 700-foot beach across from a 330-site campground.

## Wisconsin

### Door County

Located exactly halfway from the equator to the North Pole, Bailey Harbor is one of many terrfic sailing spots along Wisconsin's "thumb." Door county has about 225-miles of shoreline, from soaring granite cliffs to sand-dune-covered beaches on the Lake Michigan side.

# Lessons and Training

## *Illinois*

**Windward Sports**
3317 N. Clark
44089 Chicago, IL
(312)472-6868

**Stormy Boards**
1870 Sheridan Rd.
Highland Park, IL 60035
(312)433-8500

## *Indiana*

**Outpost Sports**
3602 N. Grape
Mishawaka, IN 46545
(219)259-1000

## *Michigan*

**Chapter 11 Sports**
114 W. Savidge
Spring Lake, MI 49456
(616)842-9244

**Bower Harbor Marine**
14039 Peninsular Dr.
Traverse City, MI 49684
(616)223-7600

**Makin Waves**
5415 W.S. 31
Acme, MI
(616)938-9283

**The Windsurf Co.**
9815 Main St.
Whitmore Lake, MI 48189
(313)449-0707

## *Ohio*

**Sailboard Alley**
101 Main
Toledo, OH 43605
(419)698-8437

**Sunports**
23 Cherri-Park Square
Westerville, OH 43081
(614)895-7873

**North Coast Windsurfing**
Route 6
Vermillion, OH
(216)967-3493

## *Wisconsin*

**Flying Fish**

600 Williamson St.
Madison, WI 53703
(608)251-4500

**Southport Rigging**
2926 75th Hwy. 50
Kenosha, WI
(414)652-3126

**Windpower**
N7351 Winnebago
Fon Du Lac, WI 54935
(414)922-2550

## Publications

American Windsurfer Magazine, Bayview Business Park #10, 21 Production Place, Gilford, New Hampshire 03246-9967.

Great Lakes Windsurfing Magazine, 1311 Bishop, Gross Point Park, MI 48230

Windsurfing Magazine (national, monthly) World Publications, 330 W. Canton Ave., Winter Park, FL 32789. (407)628-4802

Windsport Magazine (Ontario, Canada) 2409 Marine Dr., Oakville, Ontario L6L 1C6, (414)827-5462

## Organizations

Great Lakes Sailboard Association, 1311 Bishop, Grosse

Pointe Park, MI 48230, (313)885-0715.

Lansing Sailing Club, 6118 Columbia Drive, Haslett, MI 48840,

United States Windsurfing Association, P.O. Box 978, Hood River, OR, 97031, (503)386-8708.

U.S. Sailing Association, P.O. Box 209, Newport, RI 02840, (401)849-5200.

Windsurfing Canada (CYA), 504-1600 Naismith Dr., Gloucester, Ontario, K1B 5N4 (613)748-5687.

United States Professional Windsurfing Association, Bayview Business Park, Unit 10, Gilford, NH 03246, (603)293-2727.

International Women's Boardsailing Association (IWBA) P.O. Box 116, Hood River, OR 97031.

*Thanks...*

*To instructors, associations executives, enthusiasts, equip-ment manufactures, and photographers. Special thanks to Dave Sommers, Jim DuFresne, Bill Fifer, Mark van Benschoten, Six Shooter, John Heiney, Joe Boersma, Christine Uthoff, Jerry Werle, Ailes De K, Rick Bolger, John Nash, Bill Fifer, and Dan Jacalone.*